What Husbands Wish Their Wives Knew About Money

LARRY BURKETT

332.024

This book is designed for your personal reading pleasure and profit. It is also designed for group study. A leader's guide with helps and hints for teachers and visual aids (Victor Multiuse Transparency Masters) is available from your local bookstore or from the publisher.

VICTOR BOOKS ®

A DIVISION OF SCRIPTURE PRESS PUBLICATIONS INC.
USA CANADA ENGLAND

Sixteenth printing, 1989

All Scripture quotations are from the *New American Standard Bible,* © the Lockman Foundation 1960, 1962, 1963, 1968, 1971, 1972, 1973, 1975, 1977.

Library of Congress Catalog Card Number: 77-89746
ISBN: 0-88207-758-9

VICTOR BOOKS
a division of SP Publications, Inc.
Wheaton, Ill. 60187

Contents

Introduction

  1 Credit: The Great American Dream 9
  2 Credit: The Great American Hoax 20
  3 The Pressures of "Success" 35
  4 Debt Depression 49
  5 Treating the Symptoms 61
  6 Correcting the Cause 68
  7 Finding Freedom 75
  8 Establishing Plans 83
  9 Budget Breakers 97
 10 Financial Goals for Parents 113
 11 Additional Financial Goals 123
 12 Financial Goals for Children 139
 13 A Surplus: The Great Temptation 151

Introduction

"Can you help us?" pleaded Ann, a petite, 25-year-old mother of two, who had been referred to me by her pastor. As she described her situation, she frequently remarked that she just could not understand how she and her husband had gotten into such a mess. She continually asked if I could help her.

Ann's desperate statements reflect two common occurrences today: many families get into dire financial problems without realizing when and how they started; and, most people in that situation seek instant solutions.

Ann, like many others today, is a product of her training and experience. She was raised in an average American home which was neither rich nor poor. Her father was a college graduate and worked for an office supply company. He married Ann's mother when he was a junior in college and they both worked to put him through. As in most families, they lived partly on cash and partly on credit.

By the time Ann was a young girl, they were thoroughly acclimated to the use of credit cards. Though her parents were prudent and paid off their debts, they had neglected half of Ann's financial education. Ann observed her mother buying on credit but did not see her paying the credit bills.

Ann's life followed a remarkable parallel to her parents'. She married her college sweetheart, Bob, and they both worked to put him through. The only difference was that college cost a lot more for Ann's husband than it did for her father. Furthermore, credit was much more accessible to Ann and her husband.

By the time he finished school, they were engrossed in the great money game played by countless families called "Whom Do We Pay This Month?" Ann naturally thought things would get better when her husband Bob started a full-time job. But salaries for a new college graduate weren't all that good, and the demand of existing debts kept them constantly behind. However, the one benefit they did derive from full employment was more credit that allowed them to operate on "future" income.

Then five years after Ann's marriage began, it was in danger of ending. Three years of constant quarreling over money, creditor harassment over past due bills, and the endless pressures of juggling finances to make ends meet had stripped their marriage of communication and respect for one another. Instead of being companions, Bob and Ann were combatants.

Most marriages begin with the great expectations of two people who wish to share their lives together. Nearly half of these marriages fail, with miserable, bitter people the result. Why do relationships that begin with so much hope go wrong?

In over 70 percent of the marriages that fail, the primary "symptom" is finances. Under the best circumstances, conflicts between a man and a woman who share the same home are inevitable. When that relationship is strained by constant financial pressures, the result is usually open hostility, bitterness, and even divorce.

Who feels the pressure the most? Usually the wife, because her life is so intimately involved with her home. Much of her satisfaction and security comes from her home and family. Basic maternal instincts make her protective of these relationships. When her home's security is threatened, she will strike out, often in the direction of her husband. It doesn't matter that she has also contributed to the problems. Her husband is the leader and therefore, in her eyes, primarily guilty.

With rare exception, the attitudes of the woman in the family will set the stage for spending. This is not to say that husbands do not spend money: most assuredly they do. In fact, most men are far worse impulse buyers than women and will buy more expensive items. But, if the wife is a good, conservative planner, her influence on her husband will be the controlling factor. Few husbands complain that their wives are too conservative with money.

Most of you reading this book were born into a credit-oriented economy. Even if you were not "born" into it, we have all lived in this credit society for over 30 years. Therefore, most of our buying habits have been adjusted to using credit as a way of life. Just as in Ann's case, many young women have only half of a financial education. This book shares the other half with you, for I have come to believe what advertisers have long known: the wife is the key to the finances in the home.

1

Credit:

The Great American Dream

"Buy now and pay later," the advertisement says. Sounds logical, doesn't it? After all, it's not as if you can't afford it. You are simply using the item while paying for it.

"Lady, would you let your children go to school without a good set of encyclopedias?" asks the door-to-door salesman. "But how much are they?" you ask. Now what would you expect his answer to be: a simple, "Just $394"? No, instead he sneaks, "Ma'am, why they only cost 39¢ a day. That's less than a good hamburger."

What he conveniently fails to explain is that 39¢ a day, 30 days a month, 12 months a year, for seven years, is a grand total of $982.80! Plus shipping, service charges, sales tax, etc.

These sales promotion schemes and others like them emphasize the positive aspects of credit and how it is supposed to improve your lives. Unfortunately, they fail to tell the negatives: debts must be paid; most products bought on credit wear out long before the payments do; credit tempts the borrower to purchase beyond the ability to repay.

Credit: the Dream

Why do most marriages today end in separation or divorce? In over 70 percent of marriages that failed, the primary source of conflict was money. And money is what credit is all about.

In most families, credit is a constant companion of both husband and wife. In fact, few couples under the age of 30 can remember the time when credit was not the primary means of buying major appliances, automobiles, and houses. By 1980, over 80 percent of the adults in our society will not be able to recall a pre-credit economy.

The family who lives on cash-only today suffers. They are the "odd people." They have to help pay the 5% merchants pay to the credit card agencies on all credit sales. Cash buyers also help pay the built-in percentage needed for bad debts; the cost of additional personnel to process credit claims, the rental cost of the credit card impressors, and many other hidden costs of credit, including inflation resulting from the abuse of credit.

Where the Dream Begins

We are the products of our earliest training. Long after the events of youth are forgotten, the patterns that were impressed on our character will be influencing basic decisions. Childhood impressions determine to a great extent the style and color of clothes one buys. It is not surprising then that childhood observations affect one's buying habits. Given the influence of mass media advertising aimed at families for the last 30 years, it's a wonder that there are *any* families not under heavy debt burdens.

The financial world is a man's world, yet most of the buying-on-credit propaganda is aimed at women. They must, therefore, be aware of their responsibilities.

Mom is the basic teacher in the home. Children follow her leading to a great degree, especially during the first 12 years of their lives. They watch how she pays for what she buys.

Few parents would expose their children to the hazards of driving an automobile without first giving them some basic driver's training. The reason is simple. If you put a child without driving experience into an automobile, the result is predictable: disaster.

The same principle applies to handling money. We must learn to handle money properly and train our children to do so.

Basic training (called discipline) is an expression of love. When I see the misuse of money destroying a family, I often wonder why parents don't teach "credit training" to their children. Credit is as dangerous to handle as a powerful car, and should be labeled "Dangerous, Handle with Care."

Early Debt Training

Shirley was a product of early debt training. Shirley's mother loved her and never failed to give her the best even though many times she herself had to do without things. Money was never an object, not so long as Shirley's mother had her credit cards. Shirley's closet was always stocked with the latest styles from the "in" stores.

Shirley's father held a different view on credit cards. But under the barrage that her mother launched at him, he usually surrendered. Her mother compensated for their lack of companionship by dedicating herself to her daughter. Even when the creditors harrassed them about delinquent bills, Shirley's mother did not withhold from her daughter. When one card was revoked, she moved on to another.

By the time Shirley finished high school, she had her own credit cards—paid for by her mother. She lasted one year in college, slipping from the academic program to the general program and then out.

She married a boy from her hometown and settled down to married life. First, she cried and pouted her way into a new home they couldn't afford. Then she furnished it by drawing upon credit from every department store in town. Soon, Shirley's spending had exceeded not only her husband's pocketbook but her mother's as well.

Under pressure from creditors, her husband took on a second job. With mounting resentment between them, he began to withdraw from the marriage. Through all this Shirley remained aloof and unchanged. After all, she had never had to concern herself with money before, so why begin now?

The sad thing was, Shirley really loved her husband and didn't realize that her selfishness and devotion to credit was destroying their marriage. The first real shock of her life came when her husband asked for a divorce. In desperation, Shirley asked him to go with her for counseling. When the counselor asked why he wanted to divorce Shirley, he stated flatly, "I can't afford her."

Shirley found she would have to reorient her whole attitude about credit in an effort to save her marriage.

A Status Symbol

Many people in our society accumulate credit cards not necessarily to use, but to have "just in case." I recall that when I finished high school and joined the Air Force, I had no credit cards. My parents never used them, so I never had access to any. But in the service, I noticed that some of the guys in our barracks had credit cards and consequently were able to buy things I was never able to afford. They spent their pay, and still went out when the rest of us had to sit in the barracks. Their credit cards were a status symbol, and buddies collected around them for their attractive buying power.

Just as I was beginning to get a real inferiority complex, the day of reckoning came. For most of them, it was the third month of training when the bills from the first two months became delinquent and the companies wrote letters to the Air Force demanding payment. Right then, I realized it was better never to have a credit card than to face an angry sergeant who had just faced an angry colonel. For the guys whose parents wouldn't pay their debts, it meant many months of sitting in the barracks.

When I went back into civilian life, my wife and I found that we were graded by the number and kinds of credit cards we had. Just having credit cards wasn't enough. We had to have the right ones to qualify socially. The cards you could get free didn't count. The ones that charged a yearly membership fee were better. But the best were those available only if your income level was acceptable.

When my co-workers began to look on me as a little odd for not having any credit cards at all, I decided to "shoot for the sky" and get the king of credit cards, the Gold American Express. I applied for the card and was promptly turned down. I was told that $8,000 a year didn't qualify. (I often jokingly say that it was some remark I had made about buying on credit that caused an undercover credit card spy to turn me in!) So there I was, stuck with the stigma of being turned down by a credit card company, not good enough to represent their company with my money, doomed to a life of never being in debt or being able to pay 18% interest per year.

If credit was a status symbol then, it certainly is even more now. Appealing to the status motive, credit card companies hire famous actors and athletes to advertise their products, to establish a link between success and use of their card.

One recent ad said, "Not everybody can qualify for our card." It angered me because many of the couples I counsel had received one of those cards in the mail during the height of their financial difficulties. Obviously, the only qualification was to be on a mailing list.

Credit: A Necessity

"Well, you just have to have credit cards," insisted Julie when I suggested that she destroy hers. I have heard that reaction so often I would have been shocked had she not said it.

"Credit cards are a necessity in our society," she continued. "A person *must* have them. I mean, after all, you can't even get a check cashed without having credit cards in your possession."

"Julie," I answered, "I live without any credit cards and have done so for several years. I have come to realize how card-crazy we really are and

I can understand why you believe credit cards may be necessary."

For those who crave excitement, cash-only buying is the only way to live. It is always an adventure to make purchases in large stores.

Recently I was in a new department store stocking up on some automobile accessory specials. I stood in the checkout line (which was really a "credit-out" line) for nearly 30 minutes while the cashier verified card numbers, checked the bad card list, and wrote the equivalent of two novels on the vouchers. Finally I entered the home stretch, only to discover that she couldn't approve my check. I would have to go to the service desk.

So I shoved everything back into the basket and reluctantly surrendered my place in line to a credit card holder. For one fleeting moment, my courage sagged and I thought about giving up, but then I remembered all those credit card companies who would cheer at my failure, so I headed toward the service desk. Fortunately, it wasn't too crowded. There were only a few odd ones like me cashing checks.

When my turn came, the girl said, "I need your driver's license and two credit cards." I told her that I didn't have any credit cards but I did have a driver's license and a bank I.D. card (obtained as a result of many earlier battles). "Sir," she said, "you must have some credit cards. Everybody does." The way she said "everybody," I knew she meant "honest people."

"Nope," I told her, "I don't use credit cards and don't carry any either."

By this time, the store manager had come over to see what the trouble was. I went through the whole thing again with him. When he told me how sorry he was that he couldn't OK my check, I pointed to my basket and said, "Please have your stock boy return them to the shelves."

Twenty minutes later I cleared the checkout line, a little tattered, but triumphant that I had again found the soft spot in the system: a sale by check is better than no sale at all.

Credit cards are convenient, but they are a convenience many families can ill afford. Not only are credit card purchases costly if not paid on a monthly basis, but they are also costly if paid monthly. People will buy more items on credit than they will on a cash basis; they buy more expensive items; and they do less planning when using that little plastic card.

Advertising Pressure

"Go ahead and do it. You owe it to yourself," sounds good, doesn't it? If you think about it, though, this subtle bit of advertising should make you a little angry. Why? Because it implies that you are being forced to do without something that is rightfully yours.

This advertising gimmick was first pulled by a snake in the Garden. The serpent asked Eve, "You shall not eat from any tree in the garden?" (implying: "Go ahead and do it, for God is depriving you"). Unfortunately, Eve fell for it, sold Adam as well, and here we are.

The Good Life

Young couples today are faced with a barrage of advertising showing the "good" life and how credit makes it all possible. For most couples prior to the 1950s, the accumulation of a house, furniture, automobiles, and other possessions would normally be the product of 10 to 20 years of marriage. Many items were passed from generation to generation, reflecting the very attitudes of previous family owners.

Young couples today are encouraged through the use of credit to accumulate in one year what used to be accumulated in 10 years. The result? An indifferent attitude toward the cost of luxuries in the home.

Bill was a young man with a wife and young child. While Bill was in the Navy, he had inherited $12,000 from an uncle. The next 10 months of his life were filled with all kinds of goodies, including a $2,000 stereo system, a trail bike, two new cars, two skiing trips, etc.

By the time Bill was released from the service, his spending habits had settled in to indulging his twin hobbies of hunting and trail-biking. To keep up his hunting, he sold his stereo and bought a jeep and an assortment of guns, which took the last of his inherited money. Then he traded for a bigger trail bike, which put them in debt $2,000.

Within the next year, they bought new furniture (on time), a new van (to haul the trail bikes), and an assortment of expensive toys for their son. Since finances were getting a bit tight, Bill's wife went to work, which provided a new supply of money to be spent.

Three months later, they had borrowed from several finance companies, sold the jeep and trail bikes, and were still not able to meet monthly obligations.

In a little over two years, Bill and his wife had spent $12,000 in cash and were $6,000 in debt, with virtually nothing to show for it. The greatest asset they had was that they had no other source of money to tap. They were forced to face reality and learn how to handle money properly.

Is Credit Really That Bad?

Credit is not the problem. It's the lack of knowledge about credit that is the problem.

During my seminars on finances people will say to me, "It sounds like you're down on credit. Where would we be today without credit to build houses and buy cars?"

I *am* down on credit. I see the devastating effect that credit can have on a family. I also see that credit is promoted as "the great American dream," the way to buy things you can't afford.

We have an enormous government agency to tell drug manufacturers to label their products, "Danger, this product may be hazardous to your health." I believe we should advertise credit similarly, "Danger, credit may be hazardous to your marriage." Yet we ignore budget training in our schools, push credit cards into the hands of untrained consumers, and then put pressure on them to use the cards for every purchase, including groceries.

When I see so many families relying on borrowed money, I'm reminded of an old Chinese proverb, "He who rides upon the back of a tiger can never dismount."

I have heard this same frustration expressed by many families who say, "It seems like we can never get out of debt because we owe so much!"

Credit is *not* the Great American Dream. It is a cruel hoax that can destroy families if not used properly.

You and your family are not immune to financial problems. Unless you understand the complete facts and adjust accordingly, your family may be a future victim.

Women, be aware: your responsibilities are great. One of the wisest men said, "An excellent wife, who can find? For her worth is far above jewels. The heart of her husband trusts in her, And he will have no lack of gain" (Prov. 31:10-11).

2

Credit:

The Great American Hoax

When I began studying finance and economics in college, I was immediately confronted with concepts and a language I had never heard of before. I had come from an average family. My father was an employee rather than employer and was more concerned about prices in the meat market than on the stock market. Consequently, my financial education consisted of working enough on Saturday to keep my old Ford running during the week.

I naturally concluded that as some people study medicine to become doctors, I would study finance to become a financier. In college, however, instead of hearing great tips on how to become an entrepreneur, I was exposed to micro- and macroeconomics, the Keynesian theory of monetary control, and many other equally foreign subjects, each with its own vocabulary.

Not wanting to appear hickish, I drifted through

several courses memorizing what the professor said in order to repeat his words verbatim on each test. Unfortunately, they meant little or nothing to me, and thus were soon lost in the caverns of my mind. I might have drifted through my entire college career memorizing and reciting meaningless theorems had I not chosen to exchange third quarter macroeconomics for Business Finance. It was in Business Finance that I studied under my first businessman-instructor.

He often said, "Those who speak in great and glowing terms do so because they don't understand what they are talking about, and they don't want anyone else to know that they don't know."

So you *can* understand finances if you want to. Just don't be confused by people who write about finances in terms that are difficult to understand.

Early Credit

One of the common arguments for credit is, "How would we ever buy houses without credit?" It is true that few families could purchase a house today without credit. But are we to believe that credit is the great benefactor of American families because it allows them to purchase homes?

Credit isn't a new idea, of course, but the general attitude toward it is. Until recently the borrower was morally and legally bound to repay.

Psalm 37:21 defines an evil man as one who does not repay a loan. Proverbs 22:7 describes the result of excessive borrowing, ". . . the rich rules over the poor, the borrower becomes the lender's slave." This same message is repeated hundreds of times throughout God's Word. Without exception, the admonition is to avoid borrowing unnecessarily because of the dangers involved.

Until the 20th century, debt repayment was enforced stringently by the law. If someone could not repay a debt, the lender could have him thrown in prison. The lender then owned everything: the borrower's children, wife, and home. Debts were not taken lightly.

As people became more aware of the injustices of unscrupulous lenders, the laws were changed. (Unfortunately, the tactics of the lenders also changed.) The law shifted so heavily in the favor of the borrower that by the mid-1920s, he could escape even the most legitimate debts.

The Great Depression of the 1930s spelled an end to easy credit and a shift back toward lender protection. With businesses going out of existence at an alarming rate, debt enforcement laws were passed virtually unopposed. Few people noticed this change because of the drastic economic problems brought on by the Depression.

The real credit boom didn't start until after World War II. With GIs coming back from the war, there was a demand for additional housing. This demand stimulated a construction boom that was funded almost exclusively by long-term credit. Only 10 years after the war's end, 98% of all housing starts were funded by loans. Contrast this with another boom year, 1928, when only 2% of all housing starts were funded by credit.

At first, mortgages were extended for one half of the cost of the home for a period of 15 years, with an interest rate of 1-½% per year. The "average" cost of a home for a family of three was $6,500. The home mortgage consumed approximately 12% of the average family's income.

As more houses were built and more frills added, the government got involved with its seemingly limitless supply of credit. The length of mortgages increased dramatically from 15 years to 20, 25, 30, and 40 years.

With increasing competition for homes, interest rates began to rise. Once the majority of home buyers were using long-term debt, all others were forced to follow suit. Builders had to borrow for construction and add the cost to the homes. Suppliers financed inventories and passed it along. Manufacturers financed suppliers and passed the cost through. Finally, the banks borrowed additional money to lend, adding to the interest rates on new home loans.

Today, mortgage lenders add fees for closing home loans and add "discount" points to the cost of the home to compensate for long-term mortgages.

What is the net result? The average new home now requires almost 47% of the average family's spendable income. Thus, it makes a new home almost impossible for a young family and forces those who do buy into long-term financial bondage.

In the face of this, credit doesn't appear to be the American Dream. This doesn't mean that credit is the only factor in increased costs, only that it is the largest.

Adopting a "Future" Attitude

Rick and Arlene had been married about three years. Arlene had worked for a while but didn't like it, so she quit, but still filled in as a substitute teacher from time to time.

They had no particular financial problems, although an earlier cycle with credit cards during vacations had virtually eliminated any money for savings. After three years of living in apartments, they began to feel pressure to buy a house. With the advice of some friends, Rick concluded that a house would be a good investment. It certainly didn't seem to make any sense to continue pouring rent money into someone else's apartment when the money could be going into their own home.

At the time, Rick and Arlene were renting an unfurnished two-bedroom apartment for $250 a month, including utilities. They felt they could find a moderate new home for about the same cost. Reality came quickly as they began to look around. Since two-bedroom houses are not in demand, the only ones available had three or four bedrooms. In the less desirable areas the cost, when equated to monthly payments, would be at least $350 a month.

After the initial shock wore off, they calculated how much they *could* afford by scrimping in all other areas. They concluded they could afford $400 a month by cutting back on food, clothes, and non-essentials. Arlene also pointed out to Rick that he was due a raise that would help a lot.

Armed with this new estimate, they began to look more seriously. They soon found the perfect home. Set back on a wooded lot, the house looked like heaven to Arlene.

When they discussed their finances with the salesman, it became painfully apparent that they were short of the necessary down payment. Over the next few days, a solution surfaced. First, the builder would take a second mortgage for $5,000, with payments to begin in one year (out of the raise); second, little luxuries such as carpets, grass, and shrubs would be eliminated to save costs. With all of the adjustments and without the bank knowing about the second mortgage, they just qualified.

When the decision to buy was made, nothing could change Arlene's mind. Even when the salesman called to tell them that they would need to make a down payment of $2,500 before the bank would agree to the contract, an answer was found: borrow the money from her parents.

Another trauma came with closing the mortgage. The woman handling the papers told Rick and Arlene they had to pay discount points, prepaid escrow, and mortgage handling fees. These totalled nearly $1,000. Rick said no and Arlene began to cry. The result? Rick wrote a check for $1,000 on an account that had less than a hundred. By contacting his bank, Rick got the deficit added to an automatic overdraft account (at 18% per year).

A bit worse for the wear and standing in financial quicksand, Arlene and Rick finally had their "dream house," made available through the use of borrowed money.

They had hardly settled in their new home when the first problems appeared. The absence of carpets was very noticeable in a home designed for them, and the lack of a lawn made their house appear shabby. Within two months they had added carpets and drapes and planted a lawn, all on credit.

Reality surfaced again when it became apparent they could not pay their monthly bills. A few months of time were found by using credit cards for necessities, but the final blow came when Rick received his anticipated raise. Not only was it less than he expected, but it would not pay the second mortgage payment, much less the other debts. By the time the totals were assessed, their new home cost nearly $600 per month. Over 50% of their spendable income went into their "dream home."

Rick and Arlene's situation is not an isolated example. More and more families are finding that they cannot afford a new home. Those who ignore today's facts and begin to operate in the future simply find their problems more acute later.

Advertising—The Pressure to Buy

Advertising combines with credit to sell products. It does this by using four main techniques.

1. *Would you deprive your family?* This little gimmick contrasts two buyers: Fearful Freddie, who never takes a chance and therefore never provides his wife with a microwave oven or a garbage compactor; and Successful Sam, who steps out on credit and is able to provide the "better life" for his family.

2. *Sex appeal* This approach is used to promote specific product lines such as women's clothes, jewelry, perfumes, and even cars. Often it is employed by large chain stores to advertise their products. Since nobody wants to be left out or out of style, the need for these things is created. For those who cannot afford new clothes in the latest styles, the store conveniently provides credit cards.

Salespeople become so accustomed to credit card buyers that when someone pays by cash, subtle pressure is applied to encourage the cash buyer to apply for a store credit card.

3. *Super Sale—prices rolled back* Here is the ultimate woman trap: a sale item. Most stores run continual sales. Some sale items are excellent buys and can help significantly in reducing costs. Most sale items, however, are "loss-leaders," items sold at little or no profit to draw buyers into the store, particularly credit card shoppers. Since many of these sale items are inexpensive high volume goods, the merchant knows that additional purchases will be made. After all, it doesn't make much sense to charge only four or five dollars. Other nonsale

goods are combined with the sale items to increase the total.

4. *Strategic layout* Few people are aware of the science of store merchandising. The placement of items on the shelves is not by chance, nor is their location. Many surveys are run on the products women buy and the usual routes they take through the stores. Chain food stores, for instance, arrange most of the "junk" (into this group I lump candies, colas, and other assorted tasty habits) on the most convenient shelves. Many people wouldn't put those items into a full basket, but would in an empty one.

Have you ever noticed that all of the convenience foods are located between knee and shoulder height? This location is intentional—consumers don't have to strain to reach the items.

All this is not done only for credit buyers. Obviously, the system was in use long before credit cards. But it is a fact that the consumption of "junk food" has increased dramatically with the use of credit. A strategic layout system is utilized in nearly every industry that sells to home owners, particularly women.

I shared this observation with a couple and was not surprised to hear the wife refute the whole idea. Obviously, the strategy would be useless if the buyers recognized the plan, wouldn't it?

So I invited her husband to go grocery shopping with her one week. The events leading up to this decision had evolved from budget talks I had held involving buying groceries. The wife had settled on one figure for groceries and her husband on another. They compromised in the middle, and he decided to help her live within her budget.

As they entered the store, the wife selected a shopping cart and, true to habit, began to advance down the nearest aisle selecting various food items. Her husband's job was to add up the purchases on a pocket calculator. They had progressed down five of the eight aisles when he announced that they had reached their budgeted amount. Amid rigorous protests, he pushed his wife toward the checkout line and departed with the next two weeks' supply of food.

Unfortunately, the food disappeared faster than time did, and they ran out of eatables the following week. Determined to stick it out for two weeks, they consumed their stock of canned goods to stretch the meals.

Finally, it was grocery day again. This time they assaulted the store with grocery list in hand. Instead of traveling the usual route, they went down the middle aisles first. They bypassed products that were lavishly decorated as well as those for which the price was not given in comparative figures (such as 5¢ per ounce). They eliminated all paper products (except toilet paper) as well as all sugar products and prepared foods.

This time they circled the entire store and still had money left over. The agreement was that anything saved from the food budget was the wife's personal windfall. Later, this had to be modified slightly when it was found they were having more windfall than food.

Once she knew how to shop and what to avoid, this wife became an excellent budgeter. She is now a strong advocate for consumer awareness and shares ideas with other women regularly.

Why Merchants Use Credit
Most merchants accept credit cards distributed by two major credit card companies across the United

States and most of the world. These merchants pay to each card company an average of 5% of every credit sale price. They must also buy or rent card machines, maintain valid lists, and fill out detailed records in order to get paid.

Why are they willing to do this?

Though one obvious reason is that consumers want it, this is not the primary reason. With a proper advertising campaign and cash discounts, many consumers could be persuaded not to use credit cards. Why then? Because with credit, consumers will buy more often, and will buy more expensive items.

Suppose a particular chain store operates on a 10% gross profit for cash sales. Which is better, 10% of $10 million in sales, or 5% of $30 million? In reality, the difference in cost to the merchant is not significant because it is passed along to the consumer.

Many major chain stores operate their own credit system and will accept no other cards. To them, credit is a profit-making venture and may account for over *half* of their total profits.

Legalized Theft

As expensive as credit cards are, at least their cost is visible. The store pays 5% and the consumer pays approximately 18%. Thus, the total cost is 23% on time payment purchases.

Other types of credit are even worse and approach legalized theft. Small loan companies specialize in consolidating debts for overburdened families. Many of these loans are negotiated under highly emotional family circumstances at interest rates equivalent to those required by loan sharks. Few states have adequate regulations to limit or enforce interest rates charged by small loan companies.

The collection tactics utilized by these finance companies are also patterned after the loan sharks'. Many practice intimidation, harrassment, confiscation of household goods, and outright thefts. Some loan companies are oriented to overlending and are content to receive only partial monthly payments while the principal amount grows through add-on interest.

John and Ann, a couple in their mid-50s, had been burdened for several years of their marriage by various medical bills and an accumulation of credit card debts. In an effort to consolidate all of their debts, they borrowed $1,500 from a national finance company. They made the required payments on time for the first year, but in the second year there were more medical bills, so they negotiated with the finance company to make partial payments.

After several months of pressure from the finance company, they agreed to refinance the loan, lumping in the unpaid interest. Over the next few years, this routine was repeated several times. Each time the finance company secured additional assets for the indebtedness. The last refinancing had occurred three months before I met them. By this time all household goods, their car, and some family keepsakes were pledged to the debt.

I found that they had already paid 12 years on the loan at an average rate of $38 per month for a grand total of $5,472. They still owed $1,100 payable for 30 months at approximately $37 a month. If tney retired the debt at the current rate, the total paid in would be $6,572. On the original loan of $1,500, this represented a repayment of

480%, an average of nearly 30% per year in interest alone.

Automobile Loans

Most families borrow to buy a car, the second largest purchase they will make (a house is the largest). Car purchases, however, will usually consume more family dollars than a house. An average of 10 to 12 cars per family will be bought and then sold at a loss, while only two or three homes will be traded, usually at increased worth.

In general, auto loans have a unique feature. Interest is calculated on the entire amount of money borrowed for the entire period of the loan. Also, for the first third of the loan period, most of the payment goes to interest. If, after one year of a three-year loan, the buyer wishes to trade the car or pay off the loan, he or she would quickly discover that almost nothing but interest had been paid.

What is the real interest rate on a three-year auto loan? If the car is traded or refinanced after one year, about 30%; after two years, about 25%; after the full three years, about 12%.

As we will discuss later, there are ways to substantially reduce this interest burden as well as ways to reduce the actual cost of the car.

The Correct Use of Credit

Despite the unscrupulousness of some loan companies, many lending institutions are honest and sincere. Having worked with many of them on behalf of families I have counseled, I found that those in positions of authority were concerned, courteous, and willing to work out any reasonable plan to repay the indebtedness.

These companies, however, fail to establish strict controls to eliminate overborrowing. They could do their customers a great service by providing material on the correct use of credit.

Many families use credit cards as a means of bookkeeping. This usually includes charging groceries, gasoline, clothes, and other family necessities, and paying the bills monthly, so no interest is assessed.

In most instances, there is nothing wrong with doing this. But be aware that there is no correct way for the average family to use credit. Why? Because the tendency is to overbuy, to buy higher-cost items, and to do less preplanning with credit. Very few people are sufficiently self-disciplined to use credit properly. It can be done, but it requires a good budget, specific goals, and a conservative attitude.

Many people say they use credit properly by paying the accounts without interest and using the card companies as record keepers. Upon investigation it is found, with rare exception, that instead of handling credit properly, these people simply have enough income to handle credit poorly and get away with it.

Once they begin to understand when to use credit and when not to use it, a significant change comes over their attitudes.

I recall when my self-enlightenment occurred about using credit "correctly." I had counseled many "creditcardoholics" and realized that in order for them to get out of debt, they had to destroy all their cards.

To prove that living without credit cards is possible, the Lord convicted me (and I convinced my wife) to destroy all our credit cards. I had never used credit cards except for record keeping, and paid them each month, so I anticipated no great change in my financial situation.

I destroyed every card except one, which I used for travel expenses. Surrendering this last card was a great effort. Finally my wife asked me when I was going to give up my plastic idol. With that, I proceeded to cut up my last link to the credit card world and began a pay-as-you-go life.

Two significant changes came into my life. The first month that no gasoline bills or travel expenses came in, I felt as if I had been released from prison. I discovered that I had lived with the annoyance of wrong billings and credit errors so long I had forgotten how bothersome they were.

My second discovery was that I was not as prudent with my use of credit as I had assumed. I found that my total expenses dropped by at least 20%. I had not been doing enough planning for travel, as I knew I could fall back on credit cards. I also found that I had previously selected motels that took American Express and ate only in restaurants that would accept it. When I had to pay on a cash basis, I was acutely aware of costs and adopted a philosophy of getting the same value out of my first dollar spent as I would have out of my last.

Understand that I am not saying that everyone *must* live without credit cards. I know that the Lord's plan for my family doesn't include credit cards. I also know many other families who have made a decision to stop using credit cards. Once that decision has been in practice for six months or longer, the cycle is broken and credit cards are things of the past.

Credit is *not* a necessity for living. It can be

used wisely, but seldom is. It is a short-term treatment with long-range problems. In other words, it provides the means to buy without the means to repay.

Ignorance is the ally of deception. It is vital that you be *aware* of how money should be used. The writer of Proverbs said,

"By wisdom a house is built,
And by understanding it is established;
And by knowledge the rooms are filled
With all precious and pleasant riches."
(24:3-4)

3

The Pressures of "Success"

Most of us want to live peaceful and productive lives with our mates. The selection process is usually remembered as fun! With no family pressures and little worry about money, two people are free to be both friends and companions.

When the final selection is made and the decision to get married is firm, almost nothing can change it. Even parents' or relatives' arguments about the lack of money or the completion of an education have little impact. Examples of this can be found in many couples today.

"We're different, Mom. Sue and I really love each other. We'll make it," Jim told his mother. In the face of such logic, what could she do?

So Jim and Sue began preparations to be married during Jim's summer break. When Sue's mother asked her the question about how they were going to live, she retorted, "Well, Jim can work and so can I. It will really be fun." Once, during one of his frequent trips home, Jim's father suggested that he make out a budget to determine how they could "make it." He was obviously somewhat skeptical, as Jim required advances for every trip home.

Jim attempted to develop a budget, but the figures were so depressing he decided to ignore that avenue and concentrate on making plans for his marriage.

Dad, Please Send Money

Marriage for Jim and Sue began with youthful optimism. Jim worked that summer and saved enough for them to move into a campus apartment. By the time school started, Sue had found a secretarial job on campus and Jim a part-time janitorial job. With some help from their parents, they could just make it.

They were as happy as any two married people could be that first term. Jim could hardly wait for classes to end so he could get home to Sue. In fact, he directed so much attention toward her that his grades suffered greatly and he was put on probation for the next term. To get his studies back on track, they decided Jim should not work the next term. Sue would take on extra typing to make ends meet.

During the next term, Jim noticed a change in Sue's attitude. She seemed snappy and resentful and for the first time she complained about not being able to buy clothes or entertain. To make matters worse, their car broke down and she had to ask friends for rides to work. More and more, it seemed, she had to ask her father to send them money to make ends meet.

Instead of being able to stand on their own, Jim and Sue were becoming more dependent on their families. As the pressure on their marriage increased, so did their arguments. "All you ever do is complain," snapped Jim. "I seemed to get along OK before without you."

Another term went by. Jim was suspended because of low grades. Anger flared as Jim accused Sue of purposely ruining his study habits. In turn, Sue accused Jim of being a failure. The result? Two young people found themselves bitter and disgusted with marriage.

How the Pressures Begin

For many couples, the early years of marriage are the best. The lack of money seems to draw them closer to each other. Their common purpose or goal plus meager means combine to create a real sense of oneness. Unencumbered by materialism, they are free to enjoy each other mostly because there is little else to distract them. As their financial status changes, however, they shift attention from each other to outside matters.

First, the husband gets involved in his work and finds business success very satisfying. Then, the wife becomes involved with social activities, children, or her work, and they begin to drift apart. If financial pressures are generated during this period through debts, a wedge may be driven between husband and wife that can destroy their marriage. Such was the case with Larry and Jane.

Memories of Love

Larry and Jane were an "average" couple: young, talented, and unhappy. After enjoying a happy early marriage, they found financial "success" had caused their relationship to disintegrate into bitter loneliness.

Jane was both depressed and defeated. Months of constant emotional strain in her marriage had shattered her confidence and made her doubt her faith. Although she was a Christian, Jane was not experiencing much of the reward God promises. Her story seems to be an example of many families today.

Jane had helped to put Larry through college by working during his last two years. Early in their marriage, they had the kind of relationship that most young couples dream about. It was built upon trust, love, and communication.

Shortly after graduation, Larry was drafted into the service. During that time they had little or no money. In spite of that, those years were the happiest of their lives. In the evenings, they would talk for hours about the events of the day and of the plans they had for their future children, Larry's job, a home, and their lives together. Their dream was that one day Larry would own a business in which he and Jane could work together.

With no extra money, they spent their free time at the town zoo. Before Larry's tour was completed, they were on a first-name basis with most of the animals. After feeding the animals, they often would invest half of their total net worth on a hamburger shared together.

After release from the service, Larry was hired by an engineering firm as a trainee. For the next two years, he settled into the task of "getting ahead." As he got raises and promotions, Larry and Jane found they were able to buy a few previously unaffordable luxuries.

The first change in direction came after Larry was promoted to full engineer. As they began to entertain and be entertained by others in the company, Jane became aware that their furnishings didn't measure up to those of their friends. More and more she felt they had to "look successful" if they were to "be successful." As they still had very little surplus money, credit seemed to be a reasonable alternative. After all, it would be an "investment" in their future, wouldn't it?

With Jane convinced, Larry surrendered. It would be a good investment to get some of the things they needed for the future. The first investment, Larry said, had to be a car. Jane agreed, on the understanding that she could also buy some things for the house. Unfortunately, they didn't like the kind of car they could afford, so they settled on a used luxury model. Jane remodeled the living room with money borrowed from a finance company and by the time the spending spree ceased, nearly every available dollar was committed.

Then the long decline started. First, the car broke down and took extra money one month; then, the insurance came due and was slightly higher, so they dipped into their savings; then Jane got ill and had to be hospitalized. Almost without realizing it, they were under financial pressure. For the first time in their lives, Jane and Larry had an argument.

When Larry got the doctor's bill, he really blew his stack. "A $400 doctor bill, that's stupid! No doctor in the world is worth that! This has got to stop!" he shouted.

Jane retorted, "It's not my doctor bill that's the problem; it's your stupid car!"

That evening, there was another first in their lives. Larry and Jane stopped being companions and became adversaries. By the next morning, the whole thing seemed to have blown over, but that wasn't the end of it. You can be sure that this trend, once started, will progress on its own.

About three months later, the supervisor of Larry's department left to go to another company. Larry was approached about taking over his position. Larry and Jane were both ecstatic about the promotion; now he was really moving up in the company.

With the new position came $100 a month raise "Just what we needed to get out of debt," Larry chortled. The words were hardly out of his mouth when their car broke down again. This time the bill would be over a hundred dollars, according to the mechanic. "We can't afford to keep this car," Larry told Jane. "It costs to much to operate it, so let's trade for a smaller one."

"We are not buying a new car while I have to suffer with these antique appliances," Jane shouted. "I'd like to have a little help around here, too. Larry, you're just being selfish." Larry then blew up at her and they yelled at each other for the second time in their lives.

The next morning they didn't communicate much. When Larry went off to work, Jane cried most of the day. That evening, Jane told him she was sorry Larry said he was sorry, too, and that maybe there was a way they could do what both wanted. What was the solution? Buy a washer and dryer on credit payments for 24 months, and buy a car as well.

With the best of intentions, they began to look for a small, inexpensive car that fit their budget. Unfortunately for them, the small cars were placed on the lots next to full-size luxury models. After a short comparison, Larry decided the best buy would be a new car that would last longer and would save on repair bills. They traded their old car in and financed a new car for nearly three years at $100 a month. But they were both happy (at least temporarily), and seemed to have solved their differences.

About three months later, the financial pressures began to build again. Larry began to question Jane about everything she spent. They argued about groceries, light bills, dental bills, and especially cars, washers, and dryers. They began to pick each other apart. The worse their married life became, the worse their finances became, and vice versa.

They found themselves forced to borrow more money just to survive on a month-to-month basis. As one credit card came due, another would be used to pay it. Then they began to buy perishables such as food and clothing on credit and drifted deeper and deeper into debt. The more intense the pressure from debts became, the more they would argue and blame each other.

Jane began to feel relief when Larry left in the morning. This frightened her, as she realized that she was not happy around Larry anymore and actually looked forward to being away from him. Larry began to come home later and later in the evenings and would seldom communicate at all. They began to drift apart and assume an attitude of distrust.

Their marriage was becoming a battlefield. Jane would go to bed at night with a knot in the pit of her stomach and Larry went to bed with anger written all over his face. When he got paid on Fridays and tried to balance their checkbook, his anger really flared. They had checks returned for insufficient funds because Jane failed to keep good records. Creditors began calling her at home.

Fortunately for Larry and Jane, their marriage meant enough to them that they sought help. I shared with Larry and Jane over the next few months the same plan shared later in this book. It is not my plan but God's: taken from His Word, it is both simple and practical. The result of this plan in the lives of Larry and Jane was to bring them back together. Not only did they find a solution to their financial problems but also the solution to their marriage problems.

The Danger of Competitiveness

While overborrowing, lack of planning, and family strife may develop because of a lack of knowledge and proper goals, some financial problems occur because of wrong attitudes. Covetousness is one of the most devastating, usually appearing as direct competition with friends, family, and associates.

One of its effects is an incapability to establish close friendships. If a woman continually degrades friends and gossips about what they do or don't have, competition will destroy any hope for close relationships. She will often nag her husband about being a "failure." If she talks about their friends to her husband, he suspects that she will also talk about his failures to others as well. When trust and respect go out of a marriage, its days are numbered.

Marriage counselors agree that covetousness is one of the most difficult attitudes to resolve because the individual usually flatly refuses to admit that he or she is covetous.

This was the case with Joan. She and Tom had been accustomed to living in the "best" section of town, going to the best church, and being members of all the right clubs. Joan was in constant competition with her closest friends. Any time they bought anything new, Joan was sure to try to outdo them.

Tom had taken over a secure family business that paid him an excellent income. The pressure Joan applied on Tom to move up in the world eventually caused him to begin taking unwise business risks. When a friend of theirs expanded his business to several Eastern States, Joan badgered and nagged Tom about his old-fashioned ways and his lack of initiative until he agreed to expand his business as well.

During the next two years, Tom's expansion from his original two stores to over a dozen put his business, his home, and his family heavily into debt. Joan was never happier than when she would see advertisements about their growing business. The second year, Tom was named the top young businessman of the year in the city, and Joan was named chairwoman of the leading country club.

During this time, both Tom and Joan were active church leaders and were both highly in demand as speakers at Christian events. Joan was even asked to lead a women's study group on communications.

Then the bottom fell out. The economy plummeted and Tom's financial backers began to pressure him to repay some of the larger business loans. When was unable to do so, the creditors filed suit and forced him into liquidation. Tom lost the business and was also forced to sell their home.

Joan went into a shell and refused to see even her closest friends. When they needed each other the most, Tom and Joan were not even speaking.

As the business situation deteriorated even further, Tom turned his life totally over to God and turned to Joan, whom he had thought to be a more mature believer. Unfortunately, her foundation had little real structure. Instead of being a helpmate,

Joan became a tormentor. Her attitude toward Tom was disgust and rejection. Her weapons were ridicule and sex: of the first there was plenty, and of the second, none.

When they lost their home and business, Joan insisted they buy another home of comparable value. To do so, she borrowed the down payment from her family. With this social front assured, the monthly cash outgo was also assured: the private school for the kids, two new cars, the country club, and all the other amenities of success.

Under this pressure and fighting to win Joan's favor, Tom tried to start another business. He borrowed from every family member and every friend as well as every source of personal credit. But it was a hopeless venture, doomed to failure by too much debt and too much pressure. Within a few months, that business too was gone, and tremendous debts remained.

Joan's parents were paying the house payments and Tom was borrowing to keep the kids in private school. Joan had moved into another bedroom and began to voice openly her contempt of Tom's ability. Few friends were willing to associate with them because of Joan's caustic comments. No one could dare mention anyone's success in front of Joan without an instant attack about how they cheated, lied, or how she could hardly stand them because of their attitude.

The climax came when Tom refused to accept a job with Joan's father that she had arranged. Instead, he took a job with a local company owned by a close friend. The job paid enough to live modestly (without the children in private school) and to begin paying back the debts.

Joan exploded! She accused Tom of humiliating

her purposely by taking a menial job. She declared that he was not going to deprive her children and if he wanted to be a failure, he could do it alone.

The usual conclusion to situations like Joan's is divorce or mental breakdown. In this case, however, the situation turned out to be anything but hopeless. Joan found the right direction in her life by surrendering to Jesus Christ. The financial problems were cured through application of the same principles that we will later discuss.

Overcommitment to Work

Of all the problems that cause financial friction, probably none is more disheartening to a wife than a husband overcommitted to his work. Many women have said to me, "How can I compete with my husband's work? He's totally consumed by it." Unfortunately, it's true. Many men, and more recently, women, are so wrapped up in their work that they have little or no time for their families.

Usually there is a good rationalization for overwork. It may be to secure the family's future or it may be because "I want my family to have the best." Often the husband will place blame on his wife because, he says, "She just couldn't get along on any less." The truth, however, is just the opposite. Most wives would be willing to make any sacrifice to have their husbands as companions again.

But as a workaholic husband plows his life deeper and deeper into a job or business, he soon receives most of his satisfaction from work. Why? Because when he comes home he is met by a bitter, frustrated woman.

Because of her frustration with her husband, she finds herself snappy and angry with the children during the day. Yet, she knows inside that it isn't their fault, so she develops a guilt complex which makes her even more bitter toward and angry with her husband.

These attitudes manifest themselves in a variety of ways. Arguments start over trivial matters such as the husband being late for supper or forgetting an anniversary. In a marriage with balance, these matters are one source of family jokes, not warfare. A wife may go on periodic spending sprees, to punish her husband or get his attention. Some other symptoms of frustration are: unpredictable violent outbursts, threats of divorce, imagined illnesses (as real as physical ones), alcoholism, or a total dedication to outside interests. In this case, the kids are the real losers because they have neither father nor mother.

The obvious correction for this is to bring balance back into the family's life. Husbands must make a *consistent* effort to spend quality time with their wives and children and relegate their work to its proper place: after their families. If they do not, they may discover frustration culminating in divorce, separation, or some other serious marital crisis.

Such was the case with Paul when his wife Nancy told him, "Paul, I just can't take any more of your indifference. The kids and I are leaving."

Paul called to ask me to talk to Nancy. "I just can't get through to her," Paul said. "We've had fights before and she's threatened to leave, but this time she's serious."

I had met Paul and Nancy about a year earlier at a conference which I led. As always, I mentioned at the conclusion of a talk that if I could be of any service, to please let me know. Nancy did. Before I was finished, she was at the lectern requesting a counseling session. Her problem, she said, fit every aspect of a workaholic husband.

Later Nancy related the highlights of their marriage, including Paul's rapid promotions and recognition in the business world. Money was not a problem, she said. Paul provided well and they had a nice home, two cars, and, within reason, most comforts.

Nancy's problem was that she was miserable. "I married Paul," she said, "not his money. Paul's salesmen see more of him than I do."

She said they fought all the time. "I love Paul and I don't want to fight. But I get so angry inside and so lonely that, when he finally comes home, I just seem to start screaming. What really infuriates me is Paul's indifferent attitude. He tells me to stop being selfish and realize that it's his job and he *must* be gone sometimes. Gone sometimes," Nancy sobbed, "he's only *home* sometimes."

After meeting with Nancy I had a chance to meet Paul and discuss the situation. He made a temporary effort to reduce his time away from home. Unfortunately, however, he took his work home with him, so Nancy and the kids had to tiptoe around to keep from irritating him.

I had also recommended a good, Christian marriage counselor to Paul, but he flatly refused to go. He didn't have a marriage problem, he asserted. All my counsel to the contrary could not make him accept the fact that he did.

Shortly after this, Paul was promoted to area sales manager and was committed to even more work. With the excitement of a new job to satisfy him and Nancy's problem solved (or so he assumed), Paul dived right in to his new job. The result? The latest and most severe marriage crisis of his life.

As I talked with Paul and Nancy over the next few days, it was obvious that no temporary solution was going to pacify Nancy this time. The ends do not justify the means and Nancy's attitude was no better than Paul's, but she was reacting with the only defense mechanism she had left: divorce.

Faced with the certainty of losing Nancy, even temporarily, Paul saw the urgency of reordering his priorities. In his case, this mean stepping down from his position until his family was back in balance.

Over the next year, Paul and Nancy found their relationship strengthened through a common commitment to Jesus Christ. As this commitment grew, the friction in their marriage diminished. Paul came to realize that his success or failure was not related to the position he held in his company, but to the position he holds in his family.

As he has learned to love Nancy and respect her for what she is—his partner—she has learned to overlook Paul's human faults, including his need to be recognized. The result is a happy, balanced family with Christ at the center, the family next, and Paul's job running a poor third.

Not all couples are as fortunate as Paul and Nancy. Many times situations caused by workaholism drift along for many years, with subtle problems creeping in so slowly that they go almost unnoticed until some obvious external sign appears. This sign can be emotional, as we have just seen, or it can be physical, in which case many symptoms will be treated incorrectly before the real problem is uncovered and solved.

4

Debt Depression

In 1976, a well-known columnist was searching for a slogan that could best describe Americans in the bicentennial year. People submitted thousands of slogans, but the one selected as most descriptive was, "The check is in the mail."

This response points to some of the early warning signs of financial bondage in the home.

10:00 a.m. Calls

Have you ever wondered why most creditors limit the time of their collection calls to office hours, particularly between 10:00 A.M. and 2:00 P.M.? Wouldn't it seem to make more sense to put their collectors on the night shift when they could be more sure of reaching the husband? After all, the indebtedness was secured with his signature in almost every instance.

Be assured that daytime calls are not done for convenience. They are planned and calculated to achieve the desired response. Collectors know that if they can attack the pressure point in the family, she will attack her husband for them. So they call at a time when they are relatively sure of reaching the wife without the husband around. Since pressure is the tactic, the routine is repeated with increasing severity as time goes by.

Husbands, heed this warning sign: when creditors begin to call your home to pressure your wife, *you* are headed for disaster. It's time to contact those creditors and a credit counselor, if necessary, to assume your proper responsibility. Just performing a delaying routine like promising payment is not good enough. Credit agencies are immune to promises without action. For a Christian to allow this situation to exist is terrible enough, but to allow it to continue will remove any source of God's help. "Do not withhold good from those to whom it is due, when it is in your power to do it" (Prov. 3:27).

Buying Syndrome

Another sure sign of impending problems is the purchase of new items to overcome depression caused by overspending. This is not only common, but in most instances it is predictable.

When someone, often the wife, begins to feel a great deal of pressure because there is never enough money to last until the next payday, she will end up buying something new to relieve the tension. Usually, the greater the tension, the bigger the item.

Jackie and her husband Ken allowed their debts to accumulate to a point where each paycheck was a struggle to make it until the next. Ken got paid every two weeks and, by the beginning of the second week, they were down to nothing but change. They watched their spending pretty well for several months, but the pressure gradually began to bear down on them. It was always greatest when they were around friends who were financially able to do things they could not.

Finally, when the pressure seemed almost overwhelming, Ken decided that they "needed" a new car. Though Jackie didn't know how they were going to pay for it, she always accepted Ken's direction in financial matters and trusted his judgment. A close friend of Ken's who knew their financial situation tried to counsel him not to buy a new car, but Ken was obsessed with the need for something new to bolster his ego. Sound familiar? "I said to myself, 'Come now, I will test you with pleasure. So enjoy yourself.' And behold, it too was futility" (Ecc. 2:1).

I first met Ken after his friend had called to make an appointment for him. Ken had not only fallen into the trap of this rationalization once, he had tried twice. The second time came when the pressure from the new car debt got so great that they had to take a vacation to "get away from it all." It should be well understood that both the car and vacation were only temporary outlets. These and other symptoms of financial pressures should be part of an early warning system.

For Ken and Jackie, it now meant an even more difficult adjustment to correct their finances. In their case, as in every other, it meant applying the same financial cures that we will discuss later.

Self-pity

"Anxiety in the heart of a man weighs it down, but a good word makes it glad" (Prov. 12:25).

Self-pity is sometimes referred to as "the poor mouth attitude." It is characteristic of those who inwardly (and outwardly) want others to feel sorry for the plight they've gotten themselves into.

Probably very much like the previous sign, it provides a temporary outlet by talking about the problems over and over again. The fact that others feel sorry for them will provide some temporary solace. When others recognize that these individuals are seeking sympathy, rather than a change in circumstances, they must move on to new contacts.

Sympathizing with those in need of financial help can do more harm than good, particularly if there is no apparent effort for self-help. This often only delays the inevitable reckoning and ultimately makes it worse.

A few years ago, I received a call from a pastor concerning a couple he was counseling. It seems they had come to him with severe marital problems caused by heavy debts and the resulting arguments.

As the wife shared their combined problems, the pastor said he was at a loss to know how to deal with their marital problems without first dealing with the financial crisis. So he began to supply money from a church fund—first to pay the electric bill, then to make up the rent deficit. Later, it was the car and doctor bills. Before long he was supplementing their income regularly.

He noted a subtle change in their attitude as they would cancel counseling sessions and yet phone him late in the evenings, desperately seeking advice on a new crisis in their marriage. Within a few weeks, his role had been reduced to a convenient sympathizer and benefactor.

He asked for advice on what to do about his financial involvement. My answer was, "Stop the supply of free money." When he did so, they never came back for counseling again. They also stopped attending his church. The next time he heard about this couple was over lunch with an associate who was describing a problem he was having with a couple in his church. Guess who?

Physical Reactions to Money Problems
I am not a physician nor do I believe that all illnesses are caused by psychological pressures. But many are. It is interesting to note how similar many physical symptoms are among money-pressured families, especially with the women!

Prolonged Fatigue
It's not unusual for a money-pressured woman to suffer from chronic fatigue. Often it comes on so subtly that she can't remember when she began to feel tired; she just can't remember when she last felt good. She wakes up in the morning still feeling tired, and, confronted with an irritated husband, faces the day defeated before she begins.

There is always that nagging inner feeling of something wrong without being able to identify it precisely. That is, until either the creditors begin to call at 10:00 A.M. again, or her husband explodes because all the money's gone. That was Lee Ann's problem.

"How could you be so stupid?" exclaimed Ed. "Don't you ever balance that checkbook? Even a 10-year-old kid knows how to do simple addition and subtraction."

Ed and Lee Ann were not in debt, but they were still suffering under financial pressures. Ed lived in the future, always planning for a time when he *might* be unemployed or *might* be sick. So he saved and scrimped to invest every spare dollar. Lee Ann, on the other hand, didn't know a stock from a money order. She had never understood finance and truly didn't know how to balance her checkbook.

Her family life consisted of raising two children and Ed, because he was emotionally about four years old. Every time she spent a little extra money on herself or the kids, Ed would panic as if it were the last dollar in the house.

Lee Ann began to decline physically over a two-year period until she reached a stage of almost constant fatigue. She would wake up in the mornings as tired as when she went to bed. By afternoon, she felt so groggy that she couldn't concentrate, so she retreated to bed.

This routine was repeated almost every day for nearly a year. She finally told Ed that she needed to go to a doctor. Ed agreed after he found out that his company insurance would pay for most of it.

The routine was predictable with the doctor. He put her through several tests and a complete physical but could find nothing wrong with her. After a brief consultation, he prescribed some antidepressants and recommended that she seek psychiatric help.

The effect on Lee Ann was devastating. She had gone to the doctor only by badgering Ed. Now, he never missed an opportunity to remind her of what it cost. The result was that within another few months, Lee Ann was totally unable to function in her home. Finally, she attempted suicide.

Ed was shaken to his foundation. As he sought to put his and Lee Ann's life back into balance, he was confronted with the fact that his attitude about money and the resulting pressure was the cause of most of Lee Ann's problems. Through this crisis, he found the only true source of peace and protection, Jesus Christ.

Once he had found the source of inner peace, Ed's mania for "protection" disappeared and he was then able to relieve the pressure he had placed on his wife. Once freed from the constant strain she was under, Lee Ann's physical symptoms quickly disappeared.

Other Symptoms

There are many other side effects of financial pressures. While these pressures may be the result of a surplus of money, as in the case of Ed and Lee Ann, they usually occur because of excessive debts.

An early warning sign of excessive financial pressure is obsession. If your thoughts go back to your problems when you're doing something that requires considerable concentration, you probably have excessive debts. If you can't take any time off to relax without nervous tension welling up inside· same symptom. These side effects may appear when you try to read God's Word or try to pray.

If you as a wife experience these symptoms of financial pressure, you have taken a responsibility that doesn't belong to you. It belongs to your husband.

Husbands, if you don't want real trouble in your family, decide to assume your proper responsibility and eliminate both the symptoms and the problems God's way. Before we are finished, you will have the proper tools to do just that.

Marital Symptoms

A woman's reactions to financial pressures may not be physical. There are several other ways in which a wife may respond negatively to financial pressure.

Nagging When a wife is under pressure, she will often drift into a habit of nagging her spouse. She will find every little or big flaw in his character and, without realizing what she is doing, criticize his every move. Small events will be blown completely out of proportion because that internal pressure is seeking an emotional outlet.

At a retreat my wife and I attended, my attention was drawn to a certain couple because the wife seemed so unhappy. I noticed that she was careful never to touch her husband unnecessarily, and during breaks they would go off by themselves.

We made an effort to eat with them whenever possible, and began to communicate. The thing most noticeable about their relationship was the way the wife nagged her husband. She complained about his clothes, about her clothes, about his laugh, in fact, about nearly everything. As the retreat progressed, we were all challenged to confess our weaknesses and sins and ask God's forgiveness (1 John 1:9). As this young wife began to look at her own life and talk about her marriage, it was apparent that her nagging was a symptom of the pressure she was under.

They were deeply in debt and being pursued by creditors on every side. She was pregnant with their second child, and her husband had turned all the financial responsibility in the home over to her. The result? A haggard young wife showing every sign of greater problems in the future. In her own way, she was crying out for help. The key to the future for a family in this situation is: will they recognize the symptom in time to treat the problem?

Accusations It's always interesting to observe that the faults that we most readily identify in other people are those we have in our own lives.

If we have a habit of indulgence, we will harshly criticize others who display the same habit. This is particularly true if we are able to disguise our fault so that no one else knows that it exists.

"My wife just can't adjust to my new income," Jack told me during a counseling session. "In my last position, I made nearly twice as much as I do now and she just keeps on spending like she did before."

In a separate session, Jack's wife Jan had asked me to help her get Jack to stop buying such frivolous things as a new television, a new car, and a new boat, all purchased after Jack was laid off.

Even though Jack actually bought most of the new luxuries that were strapping them, he accused Jan of being frivolous. It was not until they had made a list of needs, wants, and desires purchased recently that Jack began to see that it was he, not Jan, who needed self-discipline. Jack believed that Jan could not adjust to a lower income and attempted to buy her favor. He then blamed *her* for the overspending.

Irresponsibility A nearly infallible sign of family financial problems is the husband's abdication of his position as the family financial leader.

Usually, he will juggle the books for several months while sinking deeper into the financial quagmire. If by chance his wife happens to see the overdrawn check notices or the late payment charges, he simply has to pound on his chest, make like Tarzan, and tell her, "Don't worry about it. I can handle it." Then, when all hope is past, he will either do her a favor and "let" her keep the books, or simply abandon them, knowing that her fear will cause her to pick them up. Then, what an about-face. Suddenly there should be enough money to pay all the bills and entertain as well. If there isn't? Well, obviously she isn't doing her job right. "Why, I never had that problem when I kept the books." (The lecture for the week.)

The truth is that it takes two to get into debt and two to get out. If the wife can keep records better, then perhaps she should, but only *after* the plans are made and implemented to solve the problems.

Sexual Reaction Problems brought on by financial pressures are perhaps no more evident in any marriage than in the sexual relationship.

When two people are under tensions manifested through fatigue, anger, and resentments, it is only natural that their most intimate relationship will suffer as well. Even when a couple still has good communication, financial pressures caused by debts can so occupy the wife's mind that temporary frigidity can result. If financial pressures can be lifted from the wife, even temporarily, her response to her husband will improve markedly.

If a state of tension and pressure is left in force for a long period of time, however, it can devastate the sexual aspect of the marriage.

Cold War—Hot War This sign of financial bondage is unmistakable. The cold war is normally generated when the wife gets so angry at her husband because of the mess they are in that she begins to scream at him, and he withdraws into an emotional shell. The more he refuses to communicate, the more frustrated she becomes, and the more volume goes into her voice.

"Why can't we have a few nice things like other people do?" Paula screamed. "I am so tired of never having any money to spend on this house,

I don't know what to do. Ralph, when are you ever going to make enough to get the things we need? Why do you stay with that same stupid job?"

It is little surprise that Paula was met by a notable silence from Ralph. He had already retreated into his self-image defense state: utter turnoff.

Ralph really enjoyed his job as a high school teacher. Unfortunately, it didn't pay very much at the time. As Paula realized later, it wasn't that Ralph didn't make enough; he didn't make enough to meet her expectations. Her ambitions and requirements were established by comparison, not by necessity.

Paula could take any of several alternatives to improve her home within her budget without losing Ralph's companionship. Her hot war was a sign of frustration created by artificial money pressures. Ralph's cold war was a sign of the lack of a reasonable alternative.

Once Ralph learned how to help Paula meet some of her legitimate material needs, and Paula learned what her own needs were, peace was restored and maintained.

Separation One of the last and usually most desperate signs of severe financial pressure is separation. When the finances have really gotten bad— and stay that way—many couples somehow think that if they can't solve it together maybe they can apart.

Many times this "solution" is initiated by the wife. She rationalizes her action by saying that she's trying to snap her husband out of it, to make him realize his responsibilities. Two distinct errors are made in this attempt: (1) she takes full responsibility for her act, according to God's Word;

and (2) an already dismal financial situation is made desperate by taking on two separate households to maintain.

It is true that changes must be made and the status quo is unacceptable, but escape is *never* the answer. A wise man once said, "The wise woman builds her house, but the foolish tears it down with her own hands" (Prov. 14:1). Escape merely treats the symptoms and prolongs the cure. There are many ways to treat symptoms, almost all of which sound logical at the time. They are, however, filled with pitfalls. As Solomon said, "The way of a fool is right to his own eyes, but a wise man is he who listens to counsel" (Prov. 12:15).

5

Treating the Symptoms

Why do people want to deal with symptoms rather than problems? Because relieving the symptom provides fast, temporary peace. Unfortunately, when the next symptom appears, it is usually worse than the previous one and immune to the same treatment. They are only escape mechanisms employed in an attempt to ease the pain.

Avoiding Reality
One way to relieve tension temporarily is to pretend that no problem exists. Most people who practice avoiding the reality of a situation simply seek to postpone the inevitable.

Businessmen have been known to manipulate every conceivable angle in an attempt to prolong the life of a hopeless business even one more day. Had they been asked to advise another businessman in a similar situation, they would have advised him to shut down and liquidate much earlier.

Why do people refuse to face the reality of a

situation sooner? The answer is hope: hope that some miracle will reverse the situation and bail them out.

I believe in miracles. But I have observed that God does not violate His scriptural principles to accomplish His goal; He always uses them.

Little White Lies

A common symptom is for a husband to lie to his wife about their financial situation. It may be an effort to isolate her from the problems, or fear of her reaction. He may be more likely to take either of these courses if they are suffering marital problems. In the process of trying to hide all traces of the true situation, he may borrow additional money to keep up the front, including tapping every close friend or relative.

Unfortunately, this ruse cannot be maintained forever and eventually the truth will be known. It may be the creditors hounding his wife or a series of snide comments by friends or family, but eventually the facts will surface.

When a wife has been deceived and learns the truth from a source other than her husband, the results are predictable. First, she is hurt and offended that seemingly everybody knew the truth but her. Then, she is distrustful because she wonders what else is being kept from her. In her eyes, her position in the family has been downgraded because her husband has no confidence in her. Soon, many other areas of their relationship will be questioned and an air of distrust generated.

Steve found himself in just such a position. He had borrowed money to keep his home finances going until he couldn't borrow another dime. His routine was always the same. He would use some of the money to hold off the creditors and would use most of remaining borrowed funds to invest in new "get rich quick" ventures.

Each new venture seemed to drain his resources and his ingenuity in keeping Pam unaware of their financial problems. Before his house of cards came tumbling down, Steve had accumulated over $20,000 in personal debts. It took over $3,000 a year just to pay the interest. Steve had borrowed from his family until they refused to lend him more. When the last source of credit dried up, he forged Pam's signature on some stocks that her father had given for their children.

Pam knew that Steve was under some pressure, but whenever there was a new source of money, Steve told her it was through the sale of one of his "investments."

Pam operated a small business in which she acted as a distribution center for a cosmetics company by collecting its money from local salespeople and stocking products for them. At any time she might have one to two thousand dollars on hand, of which only about 10 percent was actually hers.

One day she received a notice from the cosmetics company that her account was seriously delinquent and approximately $3,000 was due to them. Pam checked her accounts book and verified that she had asked Steve to deposit the money into a common checking account at a local bank, just as she had many times in the past. The company would then withdraw their percentage, leaving Pam with her commission.

When she called the bank, she found that the deposits had not been made for at least a month, and that the amount of money in question had been deposited into their household account. A further search of the household account showed all the money had been spent and several overdrafts issued.

By the time Steve came home that evening, Pam had discovered that he owed virtually everyone in town and was known as a "real loser."

When she confronted Steve with her discoveries, he began to unfold the whole financial mess. The more he revealed, the more Pam realized that she was probably the only person in town ignorant of the situation. To get out of the immediate crisis, Pam had to borrow the $3,000 from her brother.

After receiving their money, the cosmetics company dropped her, obviously thinking that she was no longer trustworthy.

When the dust cleared, not only was Steve left with a financial mess he had created but he also was left with a thoroughly untrusting wife as well. The conclusion to a situation like Steve's always depends on whether or not one can face his *problems* honestly and not try to escape the symptoms.

Get Away from It All
Just as many people under the pressures of financial problems will attempt to buy new things such as cars and boats to lift their spirits, many families seek to escape their present symptoms.

When finances really get tight, one of the common tendencies is to take a vacation. The logic is simple: retreat into something that will be remembered as a happy experience. On vacation, troubles are temporarily left behind. Unfortunately, those who try to avoid facing reality in this manner quickly discover that a vacation under stress is no different than a job under stress. By the time the trip is over, the symptoms are even worse.

The ultimate escape for many families is to quit their jobs and move to another area for a "fresh start." Just as in the previous circumstance, this will not help. This urge needs to be controlled and the situation faced squarely and honestly.

Bill Consolidation Loan

A family that piles up debts from many areas such as credit cards, bank loans, and finance company loans is faced with a choice: to stop the flow of credit and reduce spending to pay off the debts, or look for new sources of money.

One of these sources is called a bill consolidation loan. The purpose is to combine several small debts into one large loan so that the payments can be spread over a longer period of time, thus reducing the monthly outgo. Most finance companies encourage such loans, especially when one of their existing loans will be refinanced. Why? Because the amount refinanced includes not only principle but some of the interest as well, so they actually earn interest on the interest.

The logic behind this kind of symptom treatment sounds reasonable. It does reduce the monthly payments in most cases. Where many of the debts are on credit cards, it may actually reduce the interest paid.

But, and it is a *big* but, bill consolidation treats a *symptom*, not the problem. The symptom here is a lack of money on a month-by-month basis. The *problem* is overspending.

Unless the overspending is stopped first, the symptom of debt will return in a few months, resulting in even worse problems. The family will be trapped with all the small debts back again as well as the consolidation loan.

One "advantage" of bill consolidation loans is to provide "extra" cash. In other words, the finance company will consolidate the bills and also extend the loan to give some surplus money. Unfortunately, this only amplifies the original problem.

Often a family will use the surplus as a down payment on a large purchase (thereby incurring more debt) or put it aside as a buffer to use on monthly overspending. By the time the surplus is gone, they have adjusted spending to a higher level and are then dependent on it. Rather than adjust the spending down, they substitute credit card spending.

Back in Debt

One of the unfortunate consequences of treating symptoms is that the last case is worse than the first. During the initial dose of financial bondage, the pressure on the wife is bad. Then, there is a temporary feeling of peace when the consolidation loan looks like the answer. But when they end up deeper in debt, the effect is often amplified.

We Don't Make Enough Money

When overspending has recurred, the obvious conclusion is that there simply is not enough money.

How does a family solve that situation? By one of two methods. The husband takes on an extra job, or the wife goes to work. When a family is in financial trouble from overspending and the wife goes to work to bring in extra money, the situation seems to improve in the short run. Her income combined with her husband's provides extra income which creates a relaxed feeling and encourages more spending.

Within a few months, however, the family is deeper in debt than ever and totally dependent on the wife working. The end result? Even worse financial problems and more frustration. It should be noted that, when a wife goes to work, she will need new clothes, transportation, and lunches, and, if there are small children, she will need to pay for child care. The net result may well be additional expense, not income. In either case, without first solving the problems that have created the pressures, more money *will not help*.

6

Correcting the Cause

Few families suffer every problem previously discussed. But nearly every family suffers from *some* of the problems. Paul and Mary had made several attempts at dealing with their problems and each time found their situation worse than ever.

"You know, I really thought we had most of our problems behind us," Paul said. "Mary had been feeling much better and we were getting along better than we had in years. I don't know what happened. We determined not to use our credit cards until we had the consolidation loan paid off. But then the air conditioner broke down, and before we had that fixed, we found out that Carrie needed braces on her teeth. Then it was car tags. By the time everything leveled out again, we were out of cash and back in debt. Now Mary has had to quit her job because she can't seem to cope with both the family and work."

What had overtaken Paul and Mary was predictable to some degree. At first it was using the charge cards for the "necessary" times. Since the air conditioner repair had depleted their reserves, it was "necessary" to charge that month's gas bill. Then, the dental bills were far more than anticipated and were covered by the automatic overdraft made available through the bank.

When the car tags and insurance came due "unexpectedly," good old Master Charge came to the rescue. Now, less than eight months after Paul had taken out the bill consolidation loan, he was again faced with heavy debts.

Creditors were calling Mary at work and home. Her doctor bills were mounting again, and it took sleeping pills to turn her mind off at night. Even the mention of going through bill consolidation again caused Mary to plunge into despair.

Paul attempted to find a second job himself, but was unsuccessful. In addition, he realized that if ever he and Mary were going to have a successful marriage, he would need to spend *more* time with her and the kids, not less.

At this point, Paul and Mary had come to a crossroad in their marriage. Even if Paul could relieve the immediate pressures, they both realized that they would eventually be right back in the same situation again. As most couples do at one or more points in their married lives, Paul and Mary had to decide on their next direction.

Divorce

Many couples faced with the decision about whether to solve the problems or run, find it easier to run. They rationalize that it must be the other person's fault and that somehow the problems would miraculously disappear if they were separated. But this "solution" usually doesn't work. I have counseled many couples in their second marriages who were back in the midst of crises very similar to the ones they left.

One unique case was Dan and Mary. They had dissolved their first marriage after suffering for two years with heavy debts, creditor humiliation, and bitter arguments. After the divorce, Dan had filed bankruptcy to get out from under the burdens. During the next year, both Dan and Mary had committed their lives to Christ. They were remarried, and their marriage relationship had improved greatly during the next few months. But suddenly they realized that their finances were headed in the same old direction. They knew that if they didn't get the *right* direction this time, they would soon have another crisis on their hands.

The decision they made stopped their drift and put them on to God's plan, not just for their marriage, but for their finances as well.

Mental Illness

When living in continuing stress situations, many people become so fearful and depressed they exhibit signs of mental illness. Not everyone, of course, needs hospitalization; most simply withdraw from any responsibility and refuse to be a part of any decisions.

This form of escape, unfortunately, prevents these people from seeing their real problem—a spiritual need—the symptoms of which most doctors and counselors are content to mask through tranquilizers and antidepressants.

Harriette was an emotional invalid. She was 55 years old, divorced, and one of the most frightened people I had ever seen.

Her husband had lost a small business several years before and they had ended up in debt as a result. He had tried bill consolidation, extra jobs, and ultimately bankruptcy. When the pressure got too great for Harriette, she withdrew and refused to assume any further responsibility. She would not handle any money and refused to even discuss finances. As her fears got worse, she began to take pills for every emotion she felt, both normal and abnormal. She eventually became so worried about the future that she retreated to bed, intent on dying.

During this time, her husband moved out and later filed for divorce. This only amplified her fears and she became even more depressed. Her daughter and son-in-law came to live with her to take care of her. In a short while, they recognized that she really wasn't going to die and began to deal with her real problem—a spiritual need.

Through the help of a Christian counselor, she accepted Christ into her life. With the help of other concerned Christians, she began to meet people again and accept some responsibility for her own affairs, including finances. She has now become a productive member of her community.

The Ostrich Technique
When a family has previously attempted to treat their financial symptoms and failed to solve the problems, a great temptation is to ignore the fact that the symptoms have reappeared. People who attempt this end up in even greater trouble because creditors will not buy the ostrich method. I recognized the symptom when I answered an urgent phone call one evening.

The young man on the other end of the line said

he urgently needed help. He had just been served a "garnishment of wages" summons and was required to appear in court within five days for the judge to set the amount. His plea was, "What can I do now? I'm afraid my boss will fire me."

I asked him how old the debt in question was and when he had last paid on it. It turned out the debt was over a year old and no payment or contact had been made for nearly eight months. His reason was, "I didn't have enough money to make the whole payment every month and I didn't think they would accept a lesser amount." I then asked if he had received a copy of the original court summons when the creditor had filed suit. His reply was the same; yes, he had, but since he didn't have the money to pay the debt he simply didn't show up in court.

The old ostrich theory was working beautifully. Unfortunately, ignoring a problem will not make it go away. It always returns worse than before.

Bankruptcy

Bankruptcy is a legal means of avoiding creditors by declaring oneself to be insolvent financially.

The legal rules of bankruptcy are established by state law and thus vary from state to state, but the intent is fairly consistent. Once the court has determined that an individual owes more than he can repay, all assets are liquidated and distributed to the creditors. From that point on, no creditor may collect further payment.

Just as in the treatment of other symptoms, this escape is also temporary. Since an individual filing bankruptcy cannot do so again for six years, he is immediately supplied with readily available credit. Many times the very companies that have just lost what was owed during the bankruptcy are the first new creditors.

Religious Experience

The only true peace and fulfillment in this world comes as a result of turning one's life over to Jesus Christ. That is *not* a religious escape mechanism. It *is* a surrender of one's will and obedience to God's direction.

A religious experience, on the other hand, occurs when someone having great problems seeks escape by joining a group of people who are oblivious to any practical concern for material possessions. The result is that the financial problems are thought to be punishment for religious convictions, and therefore not worthy of further consideration.

If a woman "experiences" this change first, which is most often the case, her husband will often be subjected to a religious piousness that is almost unbearable. The attitude that seems to develop is, "I'm removed from that trivial stuff now. You take care of it."

Janet was a mother of two, slightly over 30 years old, and seemingly very religious. Her husband Jack was distraught over the fact that Janet would not accept any responsibility for finances in the home, even to the point of balancing her checkbook. Her answer for everything was, "Don't worry about it. God will provide."

God does provide; everything we have comes from Him. But He also directs us to use our abilities and to be responsible for our actions. When one turns to God for help, more responsibility is expected, not less. "And if you have not been faithful in the use of that which is another's, who will give you that which is your own?" (Luke 16:12)

Janet's actions were the reflection of an escape mechanism rather than a commitment.

Surrender to Christ

If you have never made that all-important decision of committing your life to Jesus Christ, pause a moment to consider that not to accept Him is to reject Him. "He came that you might have life and have it more abundantly" (John 10:10, paraphrased).

All He asks is that you believe in Him as your Saviour and Lord (Rom. 10:9).

If you have accepted Christ as your Saviour, have you allowed Him to be Lord over your life? You have only to yield your will to doing God's will (Rom. 12:1-2).

This is the vital step in solving family problems, financial or otherwise. The principles of handling money God's way will work for anyone, but unless this basic need is met first, the problems will appear in a different area later.

God's plan for believers here requires three basic commitments:

1. Confession: agreeing with God about disobedience and sin. This also involves a changed attitude—repentance (1 John 1:9). Without first being aware of the problems and the causes, it is impossible to effect a cure.

2. Seeking God's plan: I will outline God's plan for financial freedom for the home in the remainder of this book (Prov. 3:5-6).

3 Obedience to God's principles: A scriptural principle is God's Word applied to everyday life. Simply understanding God's plan is not enough. You must also apply it (1 John 5:3).

7

Finding Freedom

If debts, overdue bills, and depression are merely symptoms, what is the real problem?

The problem, with various alterations, is *attitude*. The attitude may be greed, covetousness, ignorance, indulgence or "get rich quick." Some people are ingenious enough to combine two or more of these attitudes, but the result is always the same: financial bondage.

Greed

Greed can be defined as always wanting more or always wanting the "best." "And all that my eyes desired I did not refuse them. I did not withhold my heart from any pleasure, for my heart was pleased because of all my labor and this was my reward for all my labor" (Ecc. 2:10).

Have you noticed that few people seem to be truly satisfied with what they have? That is why there is such a demand for bigger and shinier gadgets. Most families adjust their spending based on the availability of money, either borrowed or earned, not on needs.

Available money enables a family to expand its stock of goods far beyond what reason dictates. To verify this, one has only to shop at a few neighborhood garage sales. You will find very expensive items available for almost nothing. Why? Their owners bought them on impulse and found they had no use for them.

Famous name brands are developed to take advantage of this attitude of greed. It is interesting that men and women are willing to pay more at an exclusive shop for the same articles they could buy for much less at a good department store.

How is the attitude of greed conquered? By establishing good plans for your home according to God's principles so that you can recognize when you have enough. Jesus said, "Beware, and be on your guard against every form of greed; for not even when one has an abundance does his life consist of his possessions" (Luke 12:15).

Covetousness
The psalmist admitted to covetousness. "For I was envious of the arrogant, as I saw the prosperity of the wicked" (Ps. 73:3).

Covetousness, an attitude of desiring what others have, is what we commonly call "keeping up with the Joneses." How many times have you caught yourself comparing your success, or the lack of it, with an old school acquaintance? Or have you actually decided to change jobs or buy a larger home because your older brother was getting ahead of you?

Covetousness is promoted in most sales programs. Many sales campaigns are based on the "bait 'em and hook 'em" scheme which relies almost exclusively on greed (wanting the best) and covetousness (someone else wants it too). When a couple reads about that "great little car" in the newspaper, they hurry down to the dealer expecting to find what was advertised. "Oh, you wanted a car with engine and wheels," says the salesman, "Well, just look at this little beauty over here." So he shuffles them over to the new car section. Knowing that they came expecting to buy a car, he also knows when they spot the one they really want.

"That's *you*," he says. "You'll be the envy of your friends in this little jewel." If they hesitate or don't seem to bite right away, he will soften them up with discounts and rebates. But his clincher is, "If you really want this car, you'd better decide now. I have a guy coming in with a deposit to hold it this afternoon."

Toward what is his closing directed? Covetousness. The simple principle to employ here is: do not compare your family with others. If you do, you'll always end up in competition with someone else.

Ignorance
"The naive believes everything, but the prudent man considers his steps" (Prov. 14:15).

Ignorant does not mean stupid; it means unknowledgeable. For instance, many couples borrow money without understanding the actual interest rate. Their primary concern at the time is, "How much are the monthly payments?"

Others borrow more money than they can repay because they have no system of budgeting. They literally don't know where their money goes each month or how much credit their income can support.

I once assumed that almost everyone knew how to balance a checking account. I quickly discovered this was an erroneous assumption. Many people have only a vague idea of how much is in their bank accounts and have *never* balanced their accounts. They write checks and fail to record them in their ledger, they pay overdraft charges on checks written on insufficient funds, or they simply accept the bank's statement as totally accurate.

One couple was even paying for the bank's errors.

Cathy kept the "books" for their home records. After our first session, I had a strong suspicion that the books weren't being kept too well, as they regularly paid overdraft charges for insufficient funds. So I asked Cathy to bring her bank statement and ledger book the next visit.

A month had passed before we talked again and during that time two more checks had "bounced." I asked Cathy how she balanced her checkbook after she received the monthly bank statement.

"Oh, I look to be sure that every check they return is really ours." . . . Good, no problem there.

"Next, I cross off all the returned checks in my checkbook." . . . No problem there either, except that she forgot to mention she couldn't find all of them in her checkbook.

"Then I subtract the service charge and overdraft charges from my checkbook, deduct my outstanding checks from the bank's account, and compare my checkbook to their statement."

"Great," I said. "How do they compare?"

"Oh, they never do," replied Cathy. "So I always use the bank's figure."

Two things I discovered about this method of home accounting: (1) it is a very common method of keeping records; (2) it is grossly inaccurate.

Cathy had some enormous problems in her records. Because she didn't write down *every* check, she obviously couldn't subtract them from the bank's balance. Thus, there always seemed to be more money than there really was. We also discovered that the bank had actually paid the returned checks the first time through, added an insufficient funds penalty, and returned the check to the payee, who then resubmitted the check. By that time there were additional funds in the account and the check cleared but Cathy's account was again debited the amount of the check.

So she had actually paid the checks twice, plus penalties. When we researched the bank account, we were able to recover over $200 in overpayments during the previous year. Through this lesson, Cathy became a knowledgeable home recordkeeper. She now helps to teach other women how to manage their home accounts.

Indulgence
"He who loves pleasure will become a poor man; He who loves wine and oil will not become rich" (Prov. 21:17).

The general definition of an indulgence is "a thing that has little or no utility." It is often bought on impulse and usually stands idle after purchase.

In searching for a good example, I almost always go back to the time when I purchased a boat. I could have rented the *Queen Mary* on an hour-by-hour basis for the same use I got out of that boat. I suspect a great many men can identify with the same indulgence.

There are always good rationalizations for indulgences. How many women who purchased a bicycle slenderizing machine had first tried jogging? What usually happens to the $100 piece of equipment after it's paid for? It's stuck in the garage or basement and later sold for $5 at a garage sale. What about the great travel trailer for $3,000 that was going to save all that money on vacations? Usually used one summer, and then left to depreciate on its own. I have talked to a great many couples in financial trouble who would willingly give up their equity in boats, trailers, or motor homes, for anyone to take over the payments.

One doctor's indulgences were steam locomotives—real ones. It had all started as a hobby a few years earlier when he was collecting antique model trains. But as his involvement increased, he ran across an individual who owned an 1860 locomotive. This fellow told him what a great investment old trains were and talked him into buying his before the big steam locomotive rush got started.

So the doctor bought not one but six locomotives. He quickly discovered that owning steam locomotives is a little like catching alligators. Once you have them it's hard to let go. By the time he owned enough of them to satisfy his desire for old trains, they were draining his finances to the tune of $1,000 a month storage. After several months of fruitless attempts to sell the engines, he decided to give some away. After several months of no success at giving them away (because of the moving costs), he finally had to pay several organizations to take them.

There is a deceptively simple principle to observe concerning indulgences: Do not buy things that have little or no utility to you.

Before you buy something, identify the *need* for

the item, allocate the money for it, thoroughly search out the best buy, and pray about the purchase, giving God time to confirm or remove the desire.

Get Rich Quick

"A man with an evil eye hastens after wealth, and does not know that want will come upon him" (Prov. 28:22).

Many families have been wiped out financially because of a "get rich quick" attitude. The schemes for accommodating this attitude are as varied as human ingenuity. The common thread running through these schemes is: make a lot of money with very little effort—quickly.

Thus, the doctor is attracted to buy into an oil well, a chicken farm, or a movie. The athlete is sold a car wash franchise or the preacher a distributorship for motivational programs. The interesting common characteristic is that the get-rich-quick scheme is almost always outside of the investor's normal skill area. Then why does he get into it? Because he thinks "the grass is greener on the other side."

It is also true that many people who buy into get-rich-quick schemes risk borrowed money. Most promoters challenge prospects to borrow by attacking their reluctance as timidity. "If you don't take a chance, you'll never get ahead." It has a good ring to it, doesn't it?

One of the most far-reaching get-rich-quick programs ever created is the stock market. I don't mean to imply that everyone in the stock market is trying to get rich quick. Some people are experts and invest according to sound business and scriptural principles. But many others are involved in an area they know virtually nothing about, risking money they cannot afford to lose (often borrowed), and making decisions based on whims.

Before I am besieged by irate stockbrokers, let me say I am not debasing the stock market itself. For many wise and knowledgeable business investors, it is a useful instrument. I know many people who have made money consistently in the market. Those were the expert investors. But I have known many more people who lost money they could not afford to risk.

This same principle may apply to land syndications, fast food franchises, gold bullion, freeze-dried foods, or anything else where the product sales are de-emphasized and the get-rich-quick aspect is promoted.

How can one avoid these traps?

1. Never risk money you cannot afford to lose.
2. Never get involved with things you don't understand.
3. Demand sufficient information to evaluate thoroughly the business.
4. Seek good, noninvolved Christian counsel.
5. Set a minimum time to pray and seek God's direction.

8

Establishing Plans

There is virtually no way to avoid financial problems in the home without doing some planning.

There are two common tendencies when beginning to plan. The first is to establish plans and then never follow them. The second is to establish unrealistic plans that allow nothing for a balanced family life. Both of these lead to more frustration and eventual discouragement. Your plans must be both realistic and applied to be fruitful.

God's Part First

"Honor the Lord from your wealth, and from the first of all your produce; so your barns will be filled with plenty, and your vats will overflow with new wine" (Prov. 3:9-10).

The foundation for any family financial plan must be built upon God's Word. Throughout His Word, giving a portion of our wealth is described as essential to our receiving God's wisdom. This is *not* for God's benefit, but for ours. The willingness to surrender to God a portion of what we have is the external evidence of an internal commitment.

There will never be "enough" to give. You must simply commit that portion to God and adjust the rest accordingly. When you do this willingly and obediently, God promises to provide His wisdom to manage the rest. "There is one who scatters, yet increases all the more, and there is one who withholds what is justly due, but it results only in want" (Prov. 11:24).

Develop Good Records

It is impossible to manage your money without keeping good financial records. These include:

1. A good double entry ledger where all checks and bank expenses are posted.
2. A ledger type checkbook where *all* checks are posted when written.
3. A budget book defining the amounts to be spent on each household expense each month. This should be simple but complete. We will review the specifics of budgeting in more detail a little later.

Divide Responsibilities in the Home

It is important for both husband and wife to recognize their joint responsibilities in the home. It is sometimes taught that the home is the husband's sole responsibility. That simply is not true. God put two different people together, neither of whom is superior nor inferior, only different.

The husband is the final authority in the home, but God also assigned some responsibility and authority to the wife. If the wife in the home can manage finances better than the husband, then she ought to be the bookkeeper. In fact, wives are the bookkeepers in over 90 percent of the homes. And there is nothing wrong with this.

We must put aside once and for all this nonsense that somehow the authority in the home is undermined when the wife handles the books.

But this does not mean that when finances are in a mess the husband asks his wife to bail them out. They must both sit down, divide the responsibilities for the home finances, and decide who can best handle what. As far as contacting the creditors and working out a plan to pay, that is obviously the responsibility of the husband.

But deciding how the money should be divided into the various categories such as clothing, groceries, automobiles, insurance, etc., is a job for both husband and wife. They should create a compatible, cooperative plan, not one based on one individual's whims.

Develop a Budget

Contrary to some people's belief, a budget is not a plan by which a husband can punish his wife. A budget is a financial plan for the home.

It's interesting that none of the couples who have come to me for counseling have used a budget. Some had made out a budget and promptly filed it away in their bureau drawer. Others had made out an unrealistic budget that provided nothing for clothing, entertainment, dental or medical care, etc. It also became unusable in a very short time.

A budget is made to be used and must therefore be realistic. It should be a plan for managing *your* finances, not someone else's.

As we begin to evaluate budgets, it is important to understand the percentages given to help you evaluate your own budget. They should total 100%

or less. More than that and you qualify as "in debt."

Developing a budget means more than just writing figures down on a piece of paper. It means sitting down and talking about the current situation, where you need to go, and constructively evaluating how you are going to get there. If you have children old enough to understand, they can be included in your budget discussion.

A budget discussion must begin with the current situation. Perhaps you have never sat down and figured out how much money you make and how much you spend every month.

Most counselors have heard this response from couples who have filled out budget forms: "I know we don't spend that much money. Where does it all go every month?" A great deal of it probably goes into "Miscellaneous."

Thus, when a couple comes to me after having filled out their first budget sheet, I know that approximately two-thirds of the sheet will be accurate and one-third totally inaccurate. The first two-thirds of the sheet deals with fixed items such as the house payment, car payments, and insurance. But the last third, the miscellaneous category, deals with many variables such as food, gas, and clothes.

Often the miscellaneous category on the budget form will reflect $40-$50 a month. Experience tells me this isn't so. Nearly everyone spends more than $40-$50 a month on miscellaneous, especially those not living on a budget.

Once I have added all the figures on the expense side, I compare them with the figures on the income side. Unfortunately, there always seems to be a difference between what the figures say the couple is spending and the amount of money they are borrowing on a month-by-month basis to live. The difference is usually made up in miscellaneous. Did you ever pay off an automobile or get a raise and, without seeming to increase your spending, find that in three or four months all the money had been absorbed? Where did it go? Into "Miscellaneous."

One of the purposes of a budget is to control miscellaneous spending and evaluate where the fixed spending is excessive. There will never be "enough" money in the budget until spending is under control.

A few years ago I met a surgeon who confirmed this principle for me. He earned $180,000 a year and had done so for approximately 10 years, yet was always in debt. The doctor's early years were interesting. He had grown up in an orphanage, worked through four years of college in virtual poverty, worked four years in med school in virtual poverty, spent four years in residency training in virtual poverty, and then suddenly had an income of more than $100,000 a year.

He didn't think that anyone could spend that much money. However, anyone can spend *any* amount of money. It may take more ingenuity after $100,000, but it can certainly be done, and he proved it.

After a conference in his city, I received a telephone call from him. "The next time you are in my city, I would really like to have a chance to talk to you. I think I have a problem," he said. I asked him if he would mind describing a little bit about the problem. "Last month I made $27,000 and spent $32,000." I agreed that he really did have a problem.

A few weeks later, I was in his area and called to set up a meeting. I wanted to discern exactly what the problem was and what could be done about it. As I went through his records, I found he had his office, his home, and everything else requiring money all linked together. His receptionist, who was also his bookkeeper, paid all the bills. For the month in question, I found that he had spent $7,600 on a jeep for his son, who had wrecked it without insurance coverage, and the doctor had bought him another one. His wife had decided she wanted to grow some flowers that month, so she had a greenhouse built for $14,000. It went on and on. When I asked him about these expenditures, he said, "But that was an abnormal month. That couldn't happen every month."

As we looked back over the previous five or six months, it seemed that something equivalent had happened every month. He had so much money in oil wells that he could have bought part of Texas.

He had almost convinced me that he could control his spending without drastic measures until we walked into his back yard and I saw an airplane without wings. I asked him, "Why in the world do you have an airplane in your back yard? Does anyone in your family fly?" He said, "No, nobody flies, but a long time ago a fellow sold me that airplane because it would be a good depreciating asset." I congratulated him on the selection of that investment because it had really depreciated in his backyard.

As we began developing a budget, I found that he could have lived on $18,000 a year, and maintained the same standard of living. Obviously, he could not have bought the new cars, jeeps, greenhouses, or all the other indulgences he was involved with, including several "get rich quick" programs.

He and his wife settled on a budget of $24,000 a year. Before I left I said to his receptionist, "If he wants to get *any* more money, give me a call first."

During the next months, they lived within their budget simply by adjusting spending to the necessary rather than the lavish. After eight or nine months I received a call from the good doctor, and he was literally beaming. "I've found that we have our spending under control and three things have happened as a result. Number one, I am able to reduce the fees in my practice. Number two, we are able to have surplus money and use it for both our family and the Lord's work. Best of all though, we have peace in our lives for the first time ever."

It is equally important that you understand the purpose of a budget and adopt the budget that God plans for *your* family, not someone else's. You should also develop a realistic budget that you can live with.

After I have helped a family establish a budget, I will ask them to come back in a month or two. When they come, I ask the question, "How do you like your budget?" The response is often the same. The husband says, "Oh, I love it. It gives us more surplus money than we've ever had before." So I ask the wife, "How do you like it?" To which she replies, "It's terrible, it's so confining I can hardly stand it. I never have any free money."

I know what has happened. The husband has established a budget for his wife so confining that nobody could live with it, but he has an expense account or some other source of money to fall back on. Whenever the pressure is too great, he'll go out and eat breakfast or lunch on his expense account. Meanwhile, his wife is suffering without such a luxury. That kind of a budget will not last. It's phony.

A Budget for Me?

What then is a budget? It is simply a plan to manage the money in your home. There is nothing magical about a budget, however, and it will not work by itself. You must put it into practice.

Every area of your spending must be reviewed to determine if you are spending the correct amount. If you are not, you must decide how you can adjust it. A budget, if used properly, should help to determine what kind of a home you can live in, what kind of a car you can drive, how much insurance you should have, even what kind of clothes you wear.

Your budget should be a reflection of you. It should be a plan to bring peace, not conflict, into your home. If you as husband and wife find that you cannot create a budget and agree on it by yourselves, consult a pastor or a counselor in Christian financial service. Ask him to help you develop a budget and use him as a sounding board. "Without consultation, plans are frustrated, but with many counselors they succeed" (Prov. 15:22).

Who Needs to Budget?

Obviously, those who are in debt need to budget. Why? They're spending more than they make. The budget is a plan to balance spending with income.

Others who are not in debt also need a budget. Why? Because it's also a plan for controlling spending. A budget should help determine how much can be cut back to develop a surplus. It's that surplus that God is able to use both to enhance your life and His work.

How Much for Each Category?

I will help you go through a typical budget category by category to determine how much should fit into each one. I would suggest that you read through this entire section before you attempt to develop a budget. If, after you have finished the book you feel led to establish a budget, then do so. Come back to this section with a sheet of paper, write down each category, and make out your own budget sheet.

Step 1 List your expenditures in the home on a monthly basis.

Variable Expenses
—Food
—Outstanding debts
—Utilities
—Insurance (life, health, auto, etc.)
—Entertainment, recreation
—Clothing allowance
—Medical and dental care
—Savings
—Miscellaneous

Fixed Expenses
—Tithe
—Federal and State income tax (If these are already deducted from your pay, ignore this item.)
—Social Security taxes— treat the same as income taxes.
—Housing expense (payment/rent)
—Residence taxes
—Residence insurance
—Other expenditures that are fixed every month: car payments, payments to support family members (like Mother or Father), or any other expense that is predictable and the same each month.

Step 2 List all available income per month.

—Salary   —Interest Income
—Rents   —Dividends Income
—Notes receivable   —Income tax refund,
                            any other income.

If you operate on a nonfixed monthly income, such as sales or commissions, divide the previous year's salary by 12 to get a month-by-month budget income. Do not forget to deduct taxes and other prepayments that are due.

Step 3 Compare the categories that you've just noted as income vs. expenses. If your total expenses exceed income, you must evaluate every category to decide whether or not you are overspending and, if so, how spending can be reduced.

If your income exceeds your total expenses, you then have only to implement a plan that will help you meet your financial goals.

Step 4 Once you have established your present budget, a second budget is necessary: your "need to be" budget. In other words, now that you know how much you are presently spending, you need to decide how much you would like to spend (or can spend).

Some families may not know how much they are presently spending. In that case, I recommend that both husband and wife keep an expense diary for at least 30 or 60 days. Both should carry a small diary everywhere they go and write down all expenditures, even down to a dime.

At the end of every month, list each expenditure under the appropriate category. Then, at the end of a month or two, evaluate how much you are *actually* spending in each area. The effort of writing expenses down will probably help to control spending somewhat, but additionally, it will provide a very accurate picture of your current spending.

Bookkeeping Errors
It is impossible to have a home budget without balancing your checkbook. If you cannot balance your records, ask your bank account manager for his help. Here are some things that you should do to help keep a good checkbook:
1. Use a ledger type checkbook (as opposed to a stub type).
2. Before you tear out the first check, write in every check number.
3. Before you tear out a check, record the information in the ledger.
4. Either husband or wife should keep the ledger and the checkbook so that only one person is actually making entries.
5. Balance the ledger every month without exception.

Hidden Debts
Hidden debts usually include bills that do not come due on a monthly basis. Your budget must provide for these. If it doesn't, they will take all the surplus money for a whole month when they come due.

An example of a hidden debt is insurance that is paid on a yearly basis. The needed amount should be divided by 12 and put aside every month.

Since dental and medical bills don't come due every month, estimate how much you spend on a yearly basis, divide that amount by 12, and put aside that money every month also.

The same thing is true for clothing, automobile repairs, vacations, etc. Failure to do this will ultimately wreck your budget. Some other debts that are commonly overlooked are magazine subscriptions, credit owed to family or friends, taxes, and investments.

Impulse Items

Impulse items are the things you always wanted but never needed. As mentioned before, credit cards are the primary means of buying on impulse. Therefore, if you stop the credit, you probably stop the impulse.

Impulse purchases can be very small or very large. They range from buying homes and cars to buying lunch. The price of the object is not the important issue, its necessity is. You must consider every purchase in light of your budget.

Here are some hints on how to reduce your impulse buying:

—Use a delayed purchase plan. (Buy nothing outside of your budget unless you wait 30 days.)

—Check and record at least two other prices within those 30 days.

—Allow only one new purchase at a time on your impulse buying record.

—Never use credit cards for impulse purchasing.

I never bought large things on impulse, but the small things were still impulse purchases. Tools were my weakness. I would go into a department store and see all kinds of tools that I never needed but always wanted. Since my budget couldn't stand the strain, I decided to break the habit.

I began by posting an impulse buying chart on my bedroom door. I determined not to buy anything that cost $10 or more unless I waited 30 days and got two more prices. Also, I would not have more than one item on my list at a time. I continued that plan for over six months without purchasing a single item on my chart. The reason was obvious: once I left the store, the impulse passed, and before the 30 days was out, I'd identified something else I wanted more. Later I discovered a plan that was infallible: stay out of the stores.

Gifts

It is unfortunate that we place so much importance on gifts. But since we do, they should be a part of the budget. You should consider the amount you will spend on gifts every year and plan for their purchase.

Regardless of your financial status, in debt or otherwise, determine to bring gift giving under control. Here are a few hints that may help you:

1. Keep an event calendar during the year and plan ahead for the gifts. Buy on sale. Shop for birthdays and anniversaries ahead of time, so you don't have to buy quickly.

2. Initiate some family crafts and make some of the gifts that you need. Some of the examples are: wall plaques, purses, string art, macrame, etc. Not only will making gifts help bring your family together, but they also reflect more love.

3. Draw names for selected gifts rather than giving each family member something.

4. Do not buy gifts on credit. Credit reflects very little love. It would be much better to make something with your own hands rather than borrow in order to give.

5. Help your children earn money for gifts. You can help your children to be aware of others' needs. Perhaps rather than giving a family member a gift, they could give to someone who really needs it.

One Christmas a friend shared something that happened in his family. "The most valuable Christmas gift I ever received was a postcard from my children that read, 'Mom and Dad we love you and we've used the money for your gift to feed the poor this year. Your loving children.'"

6. Consider sending cards on special birthdays and anniversaries rather than presents. Cards reflect as much love as any other gift and sometimes more.

9

Budget Breakers

Some expenses, if not brought under control, can quickly generate debt. In this chapter we will break these critical expenses into recommended percentages of income. Be aware that percentages are not absolutes, they are only guidelines. The percentages given are based on an income of between $10,000 and $20,000 a year for a family of four. The budget has been adjusted by deducting 10% of the gross for the Lord's work and 14% for taxes. This leaves what is called net spendable income. The percentages given will equal 100% of the 76% spendable income.

Housing
"By wisdom a house is built, and by understanding it is established; and by knowledge the rooms are filled with all precious and pleasant riches" (Prov. 24:3-4).

For the salary range described above, housing should constitute approximately 30% of the spendable income. This 30% will include house payments, taxes, insurance, utilities, maintenance, and anything else associated with operating the home.

In some areas of the country, housing will cost more than the allocated 30%. It is possible to spend as much as 40% of your net spendable income and still balance your budet, if the additional amount can be gleaned from some of the other categories.

Once the expenditure for a home exceeds 40%, however, it is virtually impossible to balance the budget within the salary range presented. In this circumstance, there is probably no alternative but to move to less expensive living quarters.

Unfortunately, housing is the largest budget problem of most families, particularly young families. The average income in the United States in 1977 was $13,500. The average house in America in 1977 cost approximately $50,000. A family making $13,500 a year would have to spend approximately 50% of their income to buy a $50,000 home: virtually impossible.

It's distressing that many couples have been talked into buying a home long before they could afford it. They have neither the down payment nor the monthly payments.

What are some reasonable alternatives to buying an expensive new home? Look for an older house that can be improved by your own labor. Older houses can sometimes be purchased for much less than new ones, and family labor will enhance its worth. Look into areas that are not currently building. Areas that are building usually have plenty of traffic from people looking for homes and therefore command higher prices. Check into areas that others consider to be less desirable.

Don't be swayed by what others tell you. Make your own decisions.

Look for a small basic home that doesn't have all the frills the more expensive models do. The price of a house is increased generally because of the conveniences put into it. Select a home that suits the *needs* of your family. Don't try to plan for a lifetime in the first home you buy.

One of the best principles to observe in housing is to pray and allow God to supply the home you need at the price you can afford.

When my wife and I moved to Atlanta, we sold our Florida home where we had lived for several years. As we began to look for a house in Atlanta, I thought, "Houses just cannot cost this much." But the longer we looked, the more I realized houses really did cost that much. So we moved into an apartment.

After six months in the apartment with four growing children, we decided that we weren't cut out for that much closeness and we began to search for another home. Our search took us back to the very first house we had looked at when we came to Atlanta. It was a large home on a terrible lot. The lot was so steep that if you stood on the front lawn without baseball cleats, you would end up in the backyard.

The house was three years old but had never been lived in. So I contacted the builder to discuss his terms. He told me, "You know, I'm tired of this house. I'll sell it for exactly what it cost me to build it three years ago."

When he told me the cost, I said, "I'm really sorry, but I can't afford that. It's out of my budget." To which he replied, "Why in the world did you ask me out here to talk about the house if you can't even buy it for what it cost me three years ago?" I explained to him that I was simply being obedient to God's direction. I knew He had a house for us somewhere. All we had to do was locate it.

As we talked further, I found that he was a Christian. Before we left, he said, "Tell you what I'll do. I've been making the construction loan on this house for nearly three years myself. I'll let you rent it with an option to buy for exactly what my construction loan is."

So we moved into a home for a few dollars a month more than we were paying for an apartment. However, our apartment was about 900 square feet and the house was a little over 5,000 square feet.

We had been in the home about four months when the builder suffered a fatal heart attack. About a year later, the executor of his estate called to tell me that they needed to sell the house or they would have to pay estate taxes on it. I explained very thoroughly that I could not buy the house for what it cost to build four years earlier.

A few weeks later the executor called again to tell me that the house had been appraised for estate taxes and they would have to pay nearly the value of the house in estate taxes. I sympathized with him, but again told him that I simply could not afford the house. "It's above my budget," I said. The reply was, "Make us an offer."

I called the mortgage company where I was making the construction loan and asked them how much mortgage I could buy for what I was already paying. It turned out to be $38,000, which was promptly accepted as the purchase price of the home.

No human being could take credit for anything that happened. God understood the need in the life of the builder and matched a need in my life. God supplied more than what we could afford at a price that we could.

One of the principles a Christian should observe is: give God an opportunity to supply the things that we need within the price that we can afford.

Food

"He who tills his land will have plenty of food, But he who follows empty pursuits will have poverty in plenty" (Prov. 28:19).

Naturally an important part of a budget, food should constitute approximately 24% of our example's net spendable income. Many American families buy too much food, while others buy too little. Food is probably the most flexible part of any budget, so when overspending occurs in other areas such as housing, automobiles, or insurance, the food budget is usually cut.

The reduction of food bills requires both thought and planning. Perhaps the best planning you can do is to make out daily menus and buy food according to the menus. This requires a list of ingredients necessary for each menu and then a shopping list made accordingly.

You do not have to make 1,095 menus. The average family eats about 22 different kinds of meals. Thus, you need only about 22 basic menus listing the ingredients. The amount of food purchased is then based on nutritional requirement and not indulgence. Once you develop this habit, you'll find tremendous benefits for your family.

One of the worst things you can do is to take your children grocery shopping. A kid in a grocery store is like an octopus. Even a two-year-old child sitting in a shopping basket seems to be able to reach candies and cookies four feet away. Also, the pressures of your children will almost always force you to buy things that you otherwise would not.

Never go to the grocery store hungry. Hungry shoppers buy foods that satisfy whims rather than budgets. It's a good idea to shop food sales, particularly canned goods and bulk lot specials. In order to do this, however, there must be a surplus of money from which you can draw when necessary.

Automobiles

" 'Vanity of vanities,' says the Preacher, 'Vanity of vanities! All is vanity' " (Ecc. 1:2).

Our budget allocation for automobiles is approximately 13% of net spendable income. This percentage includes payments, gasoline, oil, maintenance, insurance, and tags: everything associated with the automobiles.

For those who are making between $10,000 and $20,000 a year, this obviously is not a lot of money. It means that they must be disciplined about automobiles. We are often unwise when it comes to our machines, particularly our cars. As mentioned earlier, many couples buy new cars they cannot afford and trade them in long before their utility is depleted.

Those who buy new cars usually keep them less than four years. In doing so they pay the highest cost possible on an automobile.

Here are a few hints on buying automobiles.

Whenever possible *save* the money first. If you obviously cannot buy for cash and must use credit, negotiate for the car on a cash basis with no trade-in. When you have settled on the price for the car, go to your own bank, borrow the money, and buy the car for cash. Then sell your old car yourself. You'll save a significant amount of money as opposed to trading in your old car and financing through the dealer. If you still owe on your old car, don't trade.

Automobile loans use something called add-on interest. The interest is calculated for the entire amount of money over the entire amount of time. The actual interest paid may be 11% to 14% per year.

There are other ways to borrow, such as loans against your savings accounts, stocks or bonds, or other assets. Such loans can often save nearly half of the interest charged for auto financing.

Decide if you need a new car, particularly a big new car. Some people, such as salesmen, need new cars frequently; most of us do not. We swap cars because we want to, not because we have to. As discussed earlier, many factors enter here such as ego, esteem, spiritual maturity, peer pressure, and common sense.

Unfortunately, few Christians seek God's will for the purchase of their cars and suffer later because of the financial strain it places on their home finances. Pray before you buy a car, seek God's direction, and let God direct you to the right car.

Debts

"Do not withhold good from those to whom it is due when it is in your power to do it. Do not say to your neighbor, 'Go and come back, and tomorrow I will give it,' when you have it with you" (Prov. 3:27-28).

Debts in the average family income should constitute no more than 7% of their net spendable income. Obviously, it would be great if most budgets had only 7% of debts or less. Unfortunately, the norm in American families far exceeds this amount.

When the amount of debt exceeds 7%, it is difficult to balance the budget. Remember that all the
percentages must add up to no more than 100%.
When two or three of these categories are over
the recommended percentage, the budget will never
balance. It means that some kind of an adjustment
must be made.

One of the most important adjustments is deter-
mining items on credit. Consumables such as food,
clothing, and gasoline, are exceedingly difficult to
repay. When they're gone, so is the desire to pay
for them. Also, since more consumables are needed,
the debts continue to pile up.

Once you have developed your budget and know
how much money is necessary for you and your
family to live on, contact your creditors. Don't
ignore them—they'll think you're dishonest.

Tell them of your situation, and then arrange
some kind of equitable payment plan.

You may have to sacrifice to get current, including reducing credit buying and seeking alternate
ways of satisfying needs. It may mean repairing
that refrigerator or washing machine that you were
going to trade. It may also mean surrendering vacation money to your creditors. Whatever you must
do to bring your debt burden back under control,
determine your priorities and stick to them.

Insurance

"A man who fails to provide for his family is worse
than an infidel, for even an infidel will provide for
those of his own" (1 Tim. 5:8, paraphrased).

Insurance should constitute approximately 6%
of net spendable income. This excludes house or
automobile insurance and includes life insurance,

health insurance, disability, etc. It is assumed here that those who have health insurance are part of a group plan.

It's unfortunate that so many American families have been misled in the area of insurance. Few couples really understand the area of insurance, either how much is needed or what kind is best. The subject of insurance will be covered more fully in a later section.

Entertainment and Recreation
"There was a certain man without a dependent, having neither a son nor a brother, yet there was no end to all his labor. Indeed, his eyes were not satisfied with riches and he never asked, 'And for whom am I laboring and depriving myself of pleasure?' This too is vanity and it is a grievous task" (Ecc. 4:8).

This portion of family expenses should constitute approximately 6% of net spendable income. We're a recreation-oriented country, and that's not necessarily bad if kept in the proper balance. But remember that those in debt should not use their creditors' money to entertain themselves. In doing so they violate the principle of paying what is due. It is a very bad witness for Christians already in financial bondage to indulge themselves at the expense of others.

Do not attempt to cut entertainment and recreation back to nothing in your budget, simply bring spending within reason. It doesn't mean that you should stop every outside activity, but it does mean that you should seek alternatives. Rather than taking a long traveling vacation, find some place closer where you can relax. One good idea is to contact another family in the area where you are going and try to arrange a swap of residences for the vacation time. If part of your family's recreation is eating out, it may mean that you must seek alternatives such as having friends in for meals. It may mean getting rid of your boat and sitting on a dock to fish.

If you are willing to seek reasonable alternatives, you can indeed find ways to reduce expenditures in this area. The Lord also knows that you need rest and relaxation. He will provide what you need when you need it.

Recently I talked with a couple who related just this. For the last three years they had been trying to take a vacation and could never accumulate enough surplus to do so. Every time they saved enough money for a vacation some expense came along that used it up. The one thing they had not done was ask God to supply what they needed.

Because it was something for themselves, they felt they shouldn't ask God for it. After we talked, they decided to place it before God and ask Him whether they should have a vacation. They regularly committed it to God for over a week. Shortly thereafter they received a phone call from a pastor in the area where they had planned to take a vacation, who asked if they would come and lead a conference in his area. When they agreed to do so, the church paid all the expenses for the entire family to go to the conference.

God provided what they could not afford at a price that they could. "Delight yourself in the Lord; And He will give you the desires of your heart" (Ps. 37:4).

Clothing
"And why are you anxious about clothing? Observe how the lilies of the field grow; they do not toil

nor do they spin, yet I say to you that even Solomon in all his glory did not cloth himself like one of these" (Matt. 6:28-29).

Clothing in the family budget should constitute approximately 5 to 7% of our example's net spendable income. Families in debt tend to sacrifice too much in this area and buy *only* in panic situations. Your family can be clothed neatly without great expense, but this requires some effort and diligence in selecting the proper clothing that your family needs.

It also requires maintenance of existing clothes when necessary. Teach your children to use their clothes properly and to carefully maintain their own clothes.

If you have children who are 13 or older, allow them to buy some of their own clothing. Give them a clothing budget, and let them select, and maintain their own clothes. You'll find there's a different relationship between young adults and clothes when they are totally responsible.

In his book *Dare To Discipline* Dr. James Dobson tells about allocating his daughters a given amount of money for clothes and allowing them to buy their own. One daughter used the money wisely, buying just the things she needed. The other daughter used her money frivolously, buying luxury items such as an expensive coat and shoes. The clothing allowances should have lasted approximately six months. But long before the six months was out, the second daughter had exhausted all her money and clothes.

Dr. Dobson related what a strain it was for him and his wife to let her go ragged for several weeks, wearing shoes and dresses with holes. But what a great lesson it was for her. She learned a practical lesson in self-discipline. The next time she had money to spend on clothing, she was a more prudent buyer.

As part of your budget planning, you should decide how much you can spend for clothing on a yearly basis, divide it by 12, and allocate that amount of money on a monthly basis. Since you will not spend the total amount of money every month you should transfer the surplus to a savings account to be available when necessary. Thus, when clothing sales are available, you will have a surplus of money from which to draw.

As you consider your family's clothing budget, ask yourself these questions: Does it really matter whether you have all of the latest styles? Do your purchases reflect good utility rather than ego? Do you buy clothes to satisfy family needs or to satisfy whims and indulgences?

Medical and Dental Expenses

"Do not boast about tomorrow, for you do not know what a day may bring forth" (Prov. 27:1).

Approximately 5% of our example's net spendable income is allocated to medical and dental expenses. There is a great advantage if you have group health insurance, but many couples do not have this benefit. Those who do not must allocate a greater amount of money in their budget. In most cases it will be far in excess of 5%.

What this means is you must reduce spending in another area of the budget to compensate. Additional expenses must be anticipated and the funds set aside regularly. Failure to do this will spoil any budget plans and lead to indebtedness.

One of the best ways to reduce medical expenses is to reduce the number of visits to your doctor.

One of the biggest problems in medicine today is that many, if not most, of the people going to doctors could have treated themselves for incidental colds, flu, or other minor illnesses. I am not suggesting that you should not go to the doctor if you're sick, but I am suggesting that you ought to decide whether your illness is severe enough to require professional medical treatment.

Practice preventive medicine. Treat your body properly with the right amount of sleep, exercise, and nutrition, and your body will respond with good health.

Treat your teeth wisely and your teeth will also respond with good dental health. Teach your children proper dental care, including the use of dental floss. If you do, you will find your expenses will drop significantly.

Another source of health comes not from a book or a doctor, but from God. If you are ill and allow Him to remove the worry and anxiety caused by finances, you will find that both your financial life and medical life will improve.

Savings

"There is precious treasure and oil in the dwelling of the wise, but a foolish man swallows it up" (Prov. 21:20).

There is nothing wrong with savings. In fact, it is a requirement for most people. The few exceptions are those people to whom God says, "Do not save, but rely on Me from day to day."

It is not unspiritual to save nor does it represent a lack of faith. Which represents better stewardship: to borrow at 18% to buy the things that wear out, or to save and then buy them without credit?

It is important that you budget some savings.

Otherwise, the use of credit becomes a lifelong necessity, and debt a way of life. Your savings will allow you to purchase for cash and to shop for the best buys, irrespective of the store you are dealing with.

Many families fail to save because they think that the amount that they can put aside is too insignificant. No amount is insignificant. Even $5 a month will help.

Those who can should establish a surplus account in an amount that will allow you to replace things like washing machines, dryers, refrigerators and the other appliances that will wear out. The savings can be any reasonable amount that fits your particular life pattern.

Be aware, however, of the difference between savings and hoarding plans. A savings plan has a specific purpose for the money being stored; a hoarding plan is money put aside for no particular reason and wouldn't be used even if needed.

During a time of recession in our country many of the debt-ridden people I counseled actually had a surplus of money in their savings accounts. I questioned them about the purpose for their savings and they said, "We're saving in case we get laid off."

Many of them were laid off and yet, instead of using their reserves, they borrowed. Why were they saving? "Just in case." Theirs was not a savings plan, it was a hoarding plan.

Years ago, if it cost $300 to take a vacation, I would save $600. But by the time vacation time came around, I had grown so attached to the $600 that I didn't want to spend it, and so I wouldn't take a vacation. That was not a savings plan, it was a hoarding plan.

One man's goal was to save up 10 years' salary so that if he wanted to take 10 years off, he could. The character of his life, however, was that if he took five days off, he got bored and would immediately go back to work. His plan was motivated primarily by fear of the future. He was doing something that had no rationale, therefore it qualified totally as a hoarding, not a savings plan.

Summary

Now you have the necessary ingredients for establishing a financial plan for your home. There is only one ingredient necessary to complete the plan —action. No plan is ever going to implement itself. It requires effort on your part and it requires good communication within the family.

Living by God's plan is not only prudent, but is also fun. If you find after establishing a budget in your home that you are under excessive pressure, then let me assure you, you probably have not adopted God's plan.

The exceptions, of course, are those who are deeply in debt and must sacrifice in order to get out. In their case, it will not be comfortable adjusting to a new kind of plan, but the peace will be worth it.

The following is a summarized list of the financial principles applicable to your home budget. Study them and then in the next chapter I will help you get started.

1. Use a written plan. The written plan for the home is called the budget.
2. Provide for God's work from the first part of your income.
3. Limit your credit. Trim back as far as possible.

4. When you are considering buying new items in your home, consider these questions before buying:
   —Is it necessary?
   —Does it reflect your Christian commitment?
   —Is it the best buy that you can find?
   —Is it an impulse item?
5. Practice saving money regularly. Even a small amount is a good discipline to establish.
6. Set your own goals with your family. Do not try to fit into someone else's goals.
7. Get out of debt. Make the commitment that you are going to get all your obligations to a current status.
8. Avoid indulgences and lavishness in your family life.
9. Seek good Christian counsel if you have a question.
10. Stick to your plans diligently.

10

Financial Goals for Parents

Every family lives at a different level. No two families are the same. No two families live in the same kind of house, drive the same kinds of cars, wear the same kinds of clothes, or eat the same food. The savings plan that would be adequate for one family will be inadequate for another. The amount of money that one family will spend on clothing will differ from the amount another will spend. So you must find a balance in your own life.

Most of that balance will be dictated by what you can afford. Another part of the balance will be dictated not only by the area in which you live, but also the neighborhood in which you live.

First, however, you must find God's plan for your life. One of the certain ways that you will know when you are living God's plan, is that you will have peace about and balance in your finances.

The Beginning
How do you begin the process of getting out of debt? As previously discussed, you must determine

how much you spend and how much you owe. Once you know exactly how much you owe, the next step is to list all your obligations, from the largest to the smallest. The total obligations will equal 100% of your debt. Determine what percentage each of your creditors represents. For instance, the largest may be 25%, and the second may be 20%, the third 15%, the fourth 10%, and so on. This determination lets you know how to allocate the funds to each creditor, which brings you to the next step.

Contact Your Creditors

You should make personal contact with every single creditor on your list. Send them not only a copy of your budget but also a copy of your breakdown so that they will know exactly how much money you can allocate to them on a monthly basis. Even though you might have been committed to paying $10, $20, or even $30 a month you can pay only what is available.

Set Some Goals

I recommend that you list each of your debts on a 3″ x 5″ card, along with the date that you committed it to the Lord. Take the smallest debt, whether it be $5 or $50, and post that 3″ x 5″ card on your bathroom mirror, so that every time you look at it you will be reminded to pray about that specific debt and do something specific and constructive about it.

Place a small can in your bedroom for the change allocated to paying off that debt, and every time you have some change in your pocket, put it in the can, and begin to reduce that debt.

Take on additional tasks as necessary to help

eliminate the debt. Consider no task too small or menial. Second Kings 5 records the story of Naaman, the leprous captain of the Syrian army who went to the prophet Elisha to be healed. Instead of going out to meet the captain, Elisha sent a messenger to tell Naaman to go down to the Jordan River and dunk himself seven times and his flesh would be restored.

Naaman was furious and stormed away saying, "Behold, I thought, 'He will surely come out to me, and stand and call on the name of the Lord his God, and wave his hand over the place, and cure the leper.'"

Then one of his servants asked him, "My father, had the prophet told you to do some great thing, would you not have done it?" And of course Naaman said yes.

Then the servant said, "How much more then when he said to you, wash and be clean." And so Naaman went down to the river, dunked himself seven times, and when he came up the seventh time, his leprosy was gone. (See 2 Kings 5:1-14.)

What is the principle in this story? Take that last debt, the smallest one, and commit yourself to paying it off by doing menial tasks for other people. It may be mowing a neighbor's lawn, cutting wood, etc. The task should be simple and humbling. Take the money and put it in the can until the debt is completely paid.

You say, "I'm not going to do that. It's demeaning and humiliating." Certainly it is. That's exactly the purpose. Several men and women have followed this direction, and every one will tell you today they will never misuse credit again. A young husband told me recently, "Every time I go into the store and think about buying something on credit, I remember mowing my neighbor's lawn or cleaning my neighbor's garage."

Obviously it's not necessary that everybody do this. The principle behind it is that you are committing yourself to a humbling task to show the Lord that you are serious about getting out of debt.

One of your greatest rewards is seeing those debts beginning to dissolve. As they do, write across your cards "An Answer to Prayer," and put them in your life notebook or prayer book. These successes will help keep your plan to recover from debt on track.

As you pay off the one debt, put the money you were paying on it into the second debt. When you have paid off the second debt, do the same for the third debt, and so on. In time you will be totally out of debt.

If you can't see a light at the end of the tunnel, remember that God can intercede on your behalf.

Several years ago I met Warren, who had just lost his real estate business. He had been in business with four other men, all of whom had taken bankruptcy. After considering bankruptcy, however, he decided that God would not allow him, as a Christian, to go bankrupt. At the time he owed over $200,000, and didn't have a job.

As we talked I realized very quickly there was nothing I could do to help him. So we stopped and began to pray. The answer to his prayer we found in Psalm 50:14-15: "Offer to God a sacrifice of thanksgiving, and pay your vows to the Most High; and call upon Me in the day of trouble; I shall rescue you, and you will honor Me."

We simply claimed that promise and prayed, "God, please rescue him."

Warren made out a budget based on the needs of his family and the needs of his creditors. Next, he contacted all his creditors, sending each one a copy of his budget. He told them that he simply did not have any money to pay them, but if they would wait, he would pay them all he could, when he could.

A miracle happened. That year, just before Christmas, one of the banks to whom he owed nearly $100,000 decided to write off his debt as a tax loss and told him not to pay it. This bank in particular was not noted for benevolence.

About nine months later, he had a second call from the same bank. One of the investments he had pledged as collateral had been sold. Not only was there enough money to pay off the indebtedness of approximately $80,000, but there was enough to yield nearly $40,000 extra.

When the other four who had been involved with the business heard about the sale, they came to him looking for a share. He told them, "If you don't share the liabilities, then you don't share in the profits." The profit from that investment got him completely out of debt.

In a little less than one year, Warren had gone from over $200,000 in debt to debt free. He continues to live on the same budget that he established during that first year. He found, as most of us do, that the high cost of living was not his problem, but the cost of living high.

But We Need Some Credit Cards

No, you do not *need* credit cards. You may want credit cards, many people desire them, but you do not need them—you *can* exist without them. For those who are in debt, it is an absolute necessity to do without them.

When I counsel a couple who have misused their

credit cards I ask them, "Are you willing to ir-
revocably commit yourself to God's supply and to
nothing else?" If they are, the cards get the old
"paper slicer treatment." As long as they are able
to borrow, they don't need to depend on God. For
a couple who has been overspending and living by
way of their credit cards, it takes a lot of courage
and faith to destroy them. But it is necessary.

If you don't have a paper slicer around your
house, and you decide to get rid of your cards, just
preheat your oven to 400° and throw them in.

Peace in Finances

Peace comes when both husband and wife work
together in making a commitment to God's way and
plan. This commitment can work out only if both
remember that their differences do not mean either
one is inferior or superior.

One of the roles of the wife in the home is that
of a counselor to her husband and children even in
finances, if necessary. Most women are not formally
trained in handling finances, but they can learn
just as well as men. In fact, women often seem to
have better balance where money is concerned.

Recently I counseled with a young couple who
were developing a budget. The husband had become enthusiastic about handling their money properly as had his wife, and he was intent on getting
out of debt. In his intensity he had decided to sell
their house and one car, cut their food budget by
half, cut out all clothing, stop all entertainment and
recreation, and take their girls out of private school.

Of course, his wife reacted negatively. That was
not at all what she intended to do and it didn't
seem reasonable. It was not reasonable. A budget
should be a balanced plan, and one that can be

used for a long period of time. This young man's plan was made in panic. His wife supplied a good balance in this case.

Many times we husbands refuse to take counsel from anyone, particularly our wives. And yet God has asked that we consider our wives as important as ourselves. "You husbands likewise, live with your wives in an understanding way, as with a weaker vessel, since she is a woman; and grant her honor as a fellow-heir of the grace of life, so that your prayers may not be hindered" (1 Peter 3:7).

Set Practical Short-range Goals

Aim toward specific goals for your family and allow time for God to change your family's attitude.

"And the seed which fell among the thorns, these are the ones who have heard, and as they go on their way they are choked with worries and riches and pleasures of this life, and bring no fruit to maturity" (Luke 8:14).

One of your goals should be to fix your spending level based on what God has supplied right now! The psalmist said, "Delight yourself in the Lord; And He will give you the desires of your heart" (Ps. 37:4). We know that God delights in doing things for us. Our problem is that we rarely allow Him to do so. Fix your spending level and allow God to do the adjusting. Rather than buying on whim, allow God to supply the things you need at a price you can afford. This is easy to do when there are no needs, but many times we crumble in the face of a crisis. Keep faith even in crises.

Goal No. 1: Trust

Recently Paul and Andrea came for counseling and one of the questions worrying Andrea was, "Our income is substantially reduced from what it was for the last few years. How will we ever buy another home? We don't even have the down payment for one."

The only answer I had was, "What a great opportunity to put your trust in God into practice. God knows your needs and specializes in the impossible. You must have enough faith to believe that if God wishes you to have a home, He will supply it."

This young couple had moved into a condominium they simply couldn't afford. The move from a $240-a-month apartment to a $600-a-month condominium had wiped out their savings and income as well. They were forced to give up the condominium and move back into an apartment. The attitude of Andrea was, "I don't think I can live in another apartment. I know we may never get another home."

We prayed about their problem, turned it over to God, and they began to search for God's direction. Before two months had gone by, they had a call from a friend who was going to India for two years as a medical missionary. He had a large home with almost every available luxury and asked if they would mind living in the house to maintain it during his absence. If they consented he would provide them with free rent. God provided a home they could never have afforded at a price they could.

Goal No. 2: Savings
The amount of money set aside in savings will vary from family to family. On an average, it will probably be between $1,000 and $1,500. This savings account can be used to purchase necessary appliances, pay for car repairs, etc.

The purpose of a savings account is not for "protection." It is to help you be a better steward of God's resources by removing the necessity for those credit cards.

Goal No. 3: Family Sharing Time

An essential part of every Christian family's growth is a family sharing time. This should be a regularly scheduled time when both husband and wife go over the financial matters of the week, including the needs of the children, the chores that were or were not accomplished, and the rewards or punishments that are going to be handed out.

Keep a chart on the specific tasks you assign your children so that each can measure his or her progress. It is also a good check of your own faithfulness in rewarding or punishing justly. You should establish the discipline that all family members will be present at the same time.

Consistency on the part of the parents is all important. If you establish 8:00 P.M. as the time to study God's Word and discuss problems, your children should recognize that their responsibility is to be there, on time! One of the ways you will know when your family time is meeting the needs of your family is when your children remind *you*.

Goal No. 4: Husband-Wife Time

As necessary as time with the children is, even more essential is time spent with your spouse. The two of you should spend time together on a regular basis, and not only after 11:00 P.M. It may mean sacrificing some outside activities, but it is vital that you begin to communicate and get to know each other. The only way to do so is by dedicating time to each other.

You should have some guidelines for your time together including specific short-range goals you're trying to accomplish.

Goal No. 5: Ministry to Other People

As your finances improve, begin a ministry to others around you. These can be your neighbors, Christian associates, or co-workers.

Show other couples the plans you have applied to your life and the effect they have had. Try to allow at least one night a month to help another couple who is having similar problems.

As you are available to others, you will find that God will bring those with needs.

11

Additional Financial Goals

So far we've been concerned with short-range planning. What about long-range planning? That is also necessary. The steps to doing so are similar to those used in short-term planning:

1. Husband *and* wife pray about their future plan together.
2. List each major decision area in your home that will directly affect your finances.
   —House
   —Automobiles
   —Job
   —Insurance
   —Savings
   —Investments
   —Retirement
   —Inheritance
3. Establish some yearly expected results and determine to review them at least once a year.

The results of this kind of preparation and planning are astounding. No longer will there be that nagging feeling of something left unfinished. It will be a time of greater understanding between husband and wife. Areas that have traditionally been sources of conflict will dissolve if, and it is a big *if*, husbands are willing to treat their wives as co-heirs and bring them into the responsibility of family planning process.

Before You Begin

Before you start long-range planning, ask yourself these questions: Are we serious? Do we sincerely want God's best in our family's finances? If so, are we willing to seek and accept God's direction? If you can sincerely answer "yes" to all these questions, you are ready to begin your personal goal planning. Necessary Planning Tools:

1. A three-ring notebook (either 8-½″ x 11″, or 5″ x 8″).
2. A double entry ledger (available from any office supply store).
3. A quiet place to do your planning.
4. A Bible.
5. Your undivided attention.

I suggest that you use the notebook exclusively for your financial planning, both short-range (budgeting) and long-range (goals).

Long-range Planning

Long-range plans will not necessarily come due within the next year but must ultimately come due. Ignoring long-range plans does not mean you will not have any. It means that you allow someone else to make your plans for you. "A plan in the heart of a man is like deep water; but a man of understanding draws it out" (Prov. 20:5).

Using your three-ring notebook, list each of the categories we will review.

Life Insurance

Life insurance *can* be a part of God's plan for our families if used correctly. It is sometimes used to "protect" the future or as a savings or retirement plan.

None of these motives, however, serves the true purpose of life insurance: to *provide* for families after the death of the income producer. When a Christian takes out enough insurance to "protect" his family from any possible contingency upon his death, it reflects an attitude of distrust toward God. God's Word provides the correct balance about "protection." "I have been young, and now I am old; yet I have not seen the righteous forsaken, or his descendants begging bread" (Ps. 37:25).

Life insurance falls into two basic categories: cash value and term.

Cash value insurance is known also as whole life, endowment, permanent insurance, or any number of other trade names. Its basic feature is that it is usually purchased for an individual's lifetime and does accumulate some cash reserve from the paid-in premium.

Cash value insurance is normally very costly in terms of the actual after-death benefit. In any family with limited funds available it represents at best a questionable purchase. At worst, cash value insurance is so costly that many families can afford only inadequate amounts. Then, when the wage earner dies unexpectedly, the family is the loser because the needed income benefits are missing.

The normal sales program for cash value is based on three promises:

1. It is "permanent" insurance and will remain in force for the individual's entire lifetime while term insurance will ultimately cease.
2. It builds a cash value that is the equivalent of a savings plan.
3. You are actually "buying" the cash value insurance while you only "rent" term.

Let's examine each of these statements from the viewpoint of the family.

What does "whole life" or permanent insurance really mean? The insurance is available for the entire lifetime of the insured, but so are the monthly premiums. Some policies can be "paid up" in a given number of years or at a predetermined age but the costs are *much* higher. Thus, the amount of money paid is about the same.

To whom does the cash value really belong? The insurance company. If the insured dies, his family receives only the face value of the policy, *not* its value plus the cash accumulated. If the cash is borrowed prior to death, interest must be paid to the insurance company. If it is not repaid prior to the death of the insured, the outstanding loan is deducted from the proceeds. Would you save with a bank that used the same rules for your savings account?

Are you actually "buying" the cash value policy? In a narrow sense only. The company pays interest on the cash "savings" which appears to offset some of the premium paid. If, however, you attempt to actually recover that money, you must pay a higher rate of interest for "your" money than the company pays you. You may be "buying" the policy but you will never "own" it.

Term insurance means insurance that is sold for a determinable number of years. Most term policies do not accumulate any cash reserves and are literally insurance only. There are two basic types of term insurance: decreasing term and level term. In decreasing term the cost (payments) stay constant but the face value or payment decreases annually. In level term the cost increases for the period selected while the face value stays the same. Simply stated:

Decreasing term = consistent cost and decreasing payout

Level term = increasing cost and constant payout

Level or decreasing term can be selected for periods of 1, 5, or 10 years.

Which insurance is best for family needs? I believe level term is better because the need for insurance in a family does not decrease at a predictable rate as the decreasing term policy does.

For example, assume that a 25-year-old father of two young children bought a $25,000 decreasing term policy. In 10 years his policy would be worth approximately $20,000 but his insurance needs would not have declined, in fact they may well have increased.

With a level term policy his premiums would have increased but the insurance coverage remained the same. Additional coverage could be purchased for the period of higher need.

Cost Comparison

Is cash value insurance actually less expensive since it accumulates a cash reserve?

It is noteworthy that most cash value policies at some point actually accumulate more cash reserves from interest and dividends paid than the yearly premiums. Does this mean the insurance is free? Not really, as this example illustrates.

Assume that a man 30 years old needs $50,000

insurance to provide for his wife and three children in the event of his death. His choices have boiled down to a cash value policy or yearly renewable term policy. The cash value policy costs $700 year.

At age 65 it will have $20,000 in cash value. If he dies any time before 65 his family will receive the $50,000 face value. Assume also that he can afford the premium. If he could not, the decision would be one of pure budget.

The term policy costs $140 per year. Each year the premium costs will increase slightly. This particular term is guaranteed renewable regardless of his health, until age 100.

The difference in premium cost between the cash value policy and term policy will be invested in U.S. Savings Bonds each year so that the equivalent of the cash value policy is being saved. At the age of 65, the cash reserves are as follows:

Cash value in insurance = $20,000

Cash in Savings Bonds = $37,000

It is also important to remember that if the husband dies before 65, his family would receive $50,000 from the cash value policy, but would receive $50,000 plus the savings bonds from the term policy.

Savings Plan

An argument for cash value policies is that they are a means of forced savings. This is true to some extent. The difficulty with using insurance as a savings plan is that if the cash value is borrowed, the policy is reduced in the event of death. Hence, the family is left without enough reserves.

Most of God's people have little reason not to be disciplined enough to save the reserves they need for emergencies. The savings in most insurance policies draws less than half the interest that can be earned elsewhere. It is a high price to pay for a lack of discipline.

Conclusions

Probably the best way to summarize life insurance by cost and type is to look at how much money is available to purchase what you need.

Most families can afford only term life insurance. Term is much less expensive than cash value insurance over an average lifetime. The older the person is when selecting insurance the more costly the term policy. But so is a cash value policy when purchased at an older age. You can get the best value by purchasing term and saving the difference. Begin an automatic purchase of U.S. Savings Bonds. They will accumulate tax-free interest until cashed.

How Much Life Insurance?

"There is a grievous evil which I have seen under the sun: riches being hoarded by their owner to his hurt" (Ecc. 5:13).

How much is enough, is a difficult question to answer precisely. There are many variables within each family that must be considered, such as: the age of the children, the wife's income capability, existing debts, current life-style and income, and any other sources of after-death income besides life insurance. One family may wish to supply enough insurance to live off interest income alone while another may wish to provide for a specific number of years. These decisions are important and should be made mutually by husband and wife.

One method to help you evaluate how much insurance you need is based on present income and spending. Once you have begun to budget and have a peace that it is God's plan for your family, the same income would probably be necessary in the event of the wage earner's death.

Using the following guide, we will assume that a man dies, leaving a wife and two young children. His annual income had been $15,000. He had no large investment plan and only a small savings plan.

Husband's income per year	$15,000
Less:	
Insurance (not necessary)	$ 250
Savings (not necessary)	600
His living costs	1,800
Social Security income	6,000
Wife's part-time income	1,200
Deducts after-death income from total deductions	($9,850)
Income needed for family	$5,150

Multiply $5,150 x 16.6 = $85,490.00 insurance needed. (Multiplying the amount needed yearly by 16.6 yields the approximate amount of insurance necessary to earn $5,150 yearly at 6% interest. Thus, the approximate amount of insurance necessary to earn $5,150 in interest income is $85,000.

If additional funds are needed for education or other special circumstances, these should also be considered. Remember that *balance* must be the key here. Trying to overprotect a Christian family can remove them from God's plan for their lives. The same God who provides for us promises to provide for our families as well. He wants us to use our sound minds to *provide* (1 Tim. 5:8) but not to try to *protect* against everything.

No Insurance?

God may direct some people not to have life insurance or any other after-death provision.

A decision to be without insurance should not be made unilaterally. Both husband and wife should be in total accord, praying about it and seeking God's peace first. If you have any doubts, go ahead and buy the insurance. You can always cancel it later if necessary.

Should Wives Have Life Insurance?

Several sales methods are used to sell insurance for women. The most common is: How much would it cost to replace the work a wife provides in the home? This is usually meant to imply a maid and other services. It seems that this reason is valid only when a family has small children and no close relatives or friends who could or would assist in the housekeeping, cooking, etc.

Another reason given for the wife to have insurance is the cost of her burial. This is a legitimate purpose to carry some insurance on a wife. Unless a family has enough money in savings to cover the funeral costs such an expense could place them in financial bondage.

My wife and I assessed this possibility in our planning and began to search for a reasonable alternative. It didn't seem to me to be good stewardship to pay out money month after month for a contingency such as my wife's possible funeral expenses.

We found an alternative through the Georgia Memorial Society (we live in Georgia). This is a nonprofit organization created to reduce the grief and cost of funerals. For a small initial fee we are guaranteed an extremely low-cost funeral for any immediate family member. The actual cost would be far less than a normal arrangement and within what I could afford. This same plan also covers all arrangements in the event of my death and removes the burden from my wife.

Memorial societies exist throughout most parts of the United States.

The principle is: If insurance dollars are limited, spend them where they are needed most, on the wage earner of the family!

Choose Your Agent Wisely

One of your best assets is a good, independent insurance agent to help you with these decisions. Shop around, a lot! Look for an agent who has your interests at heart and not his own. If you share many of the ideas that I have shared with you, most insurance agents will insist, "It isn't true." But the proof should be in black and white. Ask him (or her) to thoroughly define their insurance plan in writing and then have several other agents, including some who sell only term insurance, to give you a comparative price. Remember, "Where there is no guidance, the people fall, but in abundance of counselors there is victory" (Prov. 11:14).

Health Insurance

The matter of health insurance is too complex to do more than touch on it here. There is virtually no way to evaluate health insurance policies because each is usually tailored to individual clients or companies.

The cost of health insurance is generally excessive except for employees covered by a group (company) medical plan. For those who are not covered in this way, a major medical plan is probably best. Major medical insurance is basically catastrophe coverage. It will exclude perhaps the initial $250 to $500 of medical expenses and then pay 80% or 90% of medical expenses above the deductible. The actual cost of a major medical policy is often 30% to 50% cheaper than individual health insurance that pays after the initial $100.

With this type of insurance it is necessary that you have access to enough money to pay the deductible. Thus your long-range planning should provide savings for this purpose.

Shopping for cost and value is very important with health insurance. You will find that virtually identical policies may vary as much as 50% from one major insurance company to the next.

Disability Insurance

As with health insurance, it is almost impossible to describe the different types of disability insurance. An agent can virtually design a policy on the spot if you can afford it.

Balance is again most important. You must ask yourself whether your attitude is motivated by fear of the unknown or by God's plan for your family. A pressure salesman can generate an attitude of fear by describing "horror stories" that happened to other families. But you must develop your own plans, which may or may not include disability insurance. In no case should disability insurance be looked upon as a means to supply all future income. The cost would be so high that it would rob current family needs and even worse, take away the incentive to readjust to a new life.

Phil recently came to me asking for help in getting his home budget into shape. "I just can't seem to make ends meet," was the answer he gave to my question about his problem.

Phil was an airline pilot and made a substantial salary. It was quite sufficient to have a sizeable surplus available if handled properly. There were several areas of his budget that needed a bit more control, but the area of insurance was completely out of proportion.

He had enough life insurance to provide for two or three families in the event of his death and enough disability insurance to triple his income if he lost his pilot's license. I asked him what terrible thing would cause him to lose his pilot's license. "Would you have to suffer a heart attack or have a leg cut off?"

"No, it could be eyesight, or blood pressure, or even a loss of hearing," he said. "But if I did lose my license I wouldn't know how to do anything."

My question to Phil was, "Would you be willing to lie in bed the rest of your life with your eyes closed? If not, why plan your life as if you intend to?"

He reduced his life insurance to a reasonable amount and trimmed his disability insurance to the amount necessary for provision rather than profit. In doing so he freed almost $300 a month.

Being overconcerned about "future" protection is a common attitude held by most couples today and reflects two certainties: a good sales job by insurance agents and a believable lie by Satan. The lie really says, "You can't trust God, He won't help in time of crisis." This is not what God's Word says. Remember Psalm 50:14-15? "Offer to God a sacrifice of thanksgiving, and pay your vows to the Most High; and call upon Me in the day of trouble; I shall rescue you, and you will honor Me."

Retirement

In our society it seems that more people are worried about retiring than working. Young workers in the job market establish as their major criteria for employment job security and good retirement benefits.

Many people today work through their most productive years at a job they can hardly stand only because it has a good retirement plan. Later most of them find that retirement isn't all it's cracked up to be. There are no retirement plans that can replace 30 or 40 wasted years.

I knew an individual with a government agency whose job requirement had been eliminated for 10 years. With no job responsibilities, his single function each day was to cross off another block on his planning calendar. "One more day closer to retirement," he would say.

What a waste of life. His entire life spent in the future. Although his case is extreme, it is not unusual. Many others are falling into the trap of this same nonsense.

Before most of us who were born after 1930 are of retirement age the whole system may be drastically revised. Rather than total retirement, it will probably be necessary to adopt a modified retirement plan that will provide continuing income.

As you are considering your retirement goals you should not rob the family of current needs in prospect of some elusive "rainy day." Perhaps the following explanations of some of the more common individual retirement plans will help you decide on realistic goals.

Annuities An annuity, created specifically for retirement, is an investment plan into which the purchaser pays a scheduled amount of money into each year with the agreement that he or she will receive a lifetime income upon retirement.

The amount of payout is determined by the sum

of money paid in. For instance, a man age 30 who paid $50 a month until age 65 would naturally receive a larger annuity than a man who began paying in the same amount at age 45.

A portion of the payout is tax-free at retirement.

There are innumerable modifications available on annuities, but basically they relate to two classes of annuity: fixed and variable payout. The fixed annuity guarantees a specific amount per month from retirement age until death. The variable annuity can adjust the payout depending on the earnings of the fund from year to year.

A fixed annuity is generally better for those approaching retirement—say within 15 years—while the variable annuity is better suited for younger participants. The reason is that with the steady increase in inflation, a fixed annuity for a younger family may be inadequate by the time it matures. Thus the variable feature provides the capability to adjust with inflation.

There are also charitable annuities created by charitable organizations where a portion of the monthly installment is tax deductible and upon the death of the beneficiary the principle goes to the charity. Christians should definitely consider this as a way to invest in the Lord's work after death.

Endowment Policies This plan is similar to an annuity in that the purchaser agrees to pay a given amount per year until retirement age and in return is guaranteed a fixed monthly payout for life. This is a good deal for the issuing company because the payout is far less than the purchaser could have earned with his money invested in bank deposits.

Mutual Funds The basic purpose of a mutual fund is to combine the investment dollars of many people and buy securities in large dollar amounts.

Because of the sums of money involved, it is possible to employ expert counsel to handle the investments. Some companies charge an initial fee to handle the investment (called front loaders) while others charge a percentage of earnings. It is preferable to use a company that takes its fee from earnings. That way it assumes some risk just as the investor does.

A mutual fund is a long-range investment plan and has the capability to adjust earnings through investments in stocks and bonds (therefore losses are also possible).

Most mutual funds can be shifted from investments primarily in stocks to investments primarily in bonds. Since bonds have a guaranteed interest payout the mutual fund can therefore be converted into a relatively conservative investment.

The best advice possible is to *shop*. Check with several agents of mutual fund companies and compare their plans. You should insist that their proposals be made in writing (and in English) so that you can compare them.

There are many other types of retirement plans available including government retirement, social security, corporate security, etc. To better understand these you should ask for the appropriate brochures. If you cannot fully understand them seek counsel from someone working in that area.

Summary
"The mind of man plans his way, but the Lord directs his steps" (Prov. 16:9).

Your short-term planning is called a budget, which is a plan for controlling spending.

These are the steps in budgeting:

1. Determine how much the family is presently

spending. This may require that husband and wife keep a diary of everything spent for one or two months.

2. Establish the limits that can or should be spent for each budget category.
3. Make the necessary adjustments including moving, selling a car, etc to control spending.
4. Maintain good records for the bank account and home budget.
5. Establish a regular time for husband and wife to discuss the budget (calmly).

Husband and wife may not always agree on everything in the budget. If two people always agree on everything one of them is unnecessary. The principle to observe is: reasonable compromise. What's fair for one must be fair for the other. "Let each of you consider that others are more important than yourselves" (Phil. 2:3, paraphrase).

The steps in long-range planning are a little less precise because they involve future events such as retirement, inheritance, education, etc. But it does not mean that long-range plans are any less important. Approach each of these plans with patience and discipline. Do not let someone sell you something you do not need.

Fear of the future motivates many if not most long-range plans. That is not God's way. Husband and wife should sit down together, write out some long-range goals, pray about them, and establish some time schedules to accomplish them. Heed the Apostle Paul's words: "Be anxious for nothing, but in everything by prayer and supplication with thanksgiving let your requests be made known to God. And the peace of God, which surpasses all comprehension, shall guard your hearts and your minds in Christ Jesus" (Phil. 4:6-7).

12

Financial Goals

for Children

It's been said so many times before that it hardly
bears repeating: children are the mirrors of their
parents. The most irritating habits our kids have
are those we wish to conceal.

The way kids handle money is usually a direct
result of their early training. Too often parents go
to extremes: either lavishing gifts on their children
or depriving them of any surplus for themselves.

Where Did We Go Wrong?
Henry and Mona indulged their children with
everything their little hearts desired. Every Christmas the house was literally filled with presents for
little Hank and Ben. By the time Hank was eight
years old, he had demolished trucks, tanks, tricycles,
bicycles, train sets, phonographs, and walkie-talkies.
What do you give kids who have everything? "More
of everything" was the illogical conclusion that
Henry and Mona came to.

By the age of 10, Hank was notorious among family friends and teachers. When he didn't get his way or when others didn't jump to his every command, he would explode into violent tantrums. He pushed and shoved his way to the head of every line totally oblivious to the rights of other people. No valuables were ever safe in his possession and when other kids were exploring the world of building blocks and clay, Hank was ransacking the other kids' desks. Many teachers attempted to tell Mona about Hank, but to no avail. Whenever he was punished in school, Nancy would compensate by promising a new reward to pacify him.

When Hank joined the Little League baseball program, Mona and Henry were in their glory. Both parents had been popular in their school days, so obviously Hank would be too. Typically, Hank would not accept instruction or discipline, so consequently he didn't make the first team. But the next year, Henry managed the team and Hank made first team. At the end of the season, Mona gave the whole team trophies, a big swimming party, a banquet, and a plasticized picture. Without even trying, Hank had been elevated to a position where no future rewards were interesting.

The first real shock came when Hank was 13. His conduct around home became strange and he was often moody and sullen. Mona later found alcohol and drugs hidden in his room. When Henry confronted his son, he was met by a barrage of foul language and declarations of what he could do with his job and reputation.

This whole mess was not entirely created by these parents spoiling Hank, but a great deal of it was. They had so indulged their son that he had little or no ambition by the time he was a teenager.

They had used their son. Hank became a little alter ego for the parents and ultimately turned on them.

If Henry and Mona loved their kids (and they did), they failed to show it in the proper fashion. They never disciplined their sons, yet they expected respect from them. They sowed seeds of selfishness and reaped a crop of bitterness.

Children need to know their boundaries. They even desire them. When none are established, they feel insecure and fearful. The usual result is an imbalanced life and wrong attitudes. When everything is attained without effort, neither material nor social values are cherished.

Who—My Son?

It is important to establish financial boundaries for children as early as possible. Many—even most—parents today complain that their children are lazy around their home. The truth is, most children are effectively trained to be lazy and undisciplined, specifically in their handling of money. No, not purposefully: by default. Most parents fail to establish work routines for their children, and those who do rarely stick to them.

Kids continually probe their environment and confines to see how elastic they are. When they find a soft spot, they push to see how far they can go before disobedience meets punishment.

With money, it is no different. First, little Timmy discovers the correlation between the jingle of the bicycle bell and the ice-cream man. When he is very young, his excitement and cute little "Icethim, Mommy, icethim," are rewarded with a quarter for ice cream. Later, when he is not quite so cute, he resorts to a screaming fit, which is rewarded in the same way as his earlier technique. Finally, little

Timmy is an adolescent who refuses (or skillfully avoids) any responsibility around home because he knows he can talk Mom out of the money he needs.

Most parents of these sullen, sluggish monsters are surprised to discover that when their "lazy" kids are exposed to stern discipline and adequate rewards, they become hard working, loyal employees.

Our son, Danny, was a classic modern adolescent whose attitude about money was "Gimme." His room was more of a mess than the average auto junkyard and would have qualified as a "disaster" area. After several attempts to get him to clean his den, my wife would resort to her ultimate threat, "I'll let your father handle this." When forced out of his den to perform some heroic act like raking the lawn, he would grumble and kick a few leaves around then quietly slip out of voice range. My usual method of correction was punitive. I would strip him of all activities and place additional work on him.

This master-slave relationship didn't seem to be the most effective plan because both he and I were constantly frustrated. Then, at the age of 13, a friend of ours asked us if Danny would be interested in splitting some wood for them in preparation for winter. Not wishing to lose a good friend, I forewarned him that Danny was not the most dependable worker around. So warned, our friend decided that Danny should be paid by the job and not by the hour.

The next weekend, Danny went to their home to work at his first real job. In less than four hours he had reduced their entire stock of logs to fireplace-sized pieces. My friend remarked how Danny would not stop for anything until he had completed his task. He then congratulated me on raising such a diligent young worker.

I was floored! What was the magic that had transformed my seemingly lazy son into a veritable Paul Bunyan? Was it just the money? I didn't think so, because I had already tried to bribe him into working, but to little avail. What then was the secret of his sudden turn-around? I knew if I could discover it and repeat the process, thousands of grateful parents would thank me.

It was not until several months later that the real answer came to me: trust and praise. I had attempted to teach my son diligence through discipline, which was partially effective; then through bribes, which was ineffective; and finally through anger, which was destructive.

What my friend had done inadvertently was reward him through *trust* and praise. He had asked him to do a man's job and, because he wasn't related, expected him to perform like a man. It never occurred to him to remind Danny three or four times to do the job right and to be careful of his tools. He also neglected to tear down Danny's self-image by assuming that he would goof off and attempt to sneak away. He defined the task, agreed on the reward, and entrusted the job to Danny.

If Danny could be motivated so simply, I thought, why not continue a good thing? Thus, we began to direct our son through *trust* and praise, expecting results according to his ability and praising his achievements. Changes began to occur as we applied these and other ideas from God's Word.

Needs, Wants, and Desires

Many parents today practice *saturation* training on their children, lavishing gifts and rewards without merit on them. In spite of all the teaching in Scripture to the contrary, we still have the notion that we can direct our children through indulgence. It simply doesn't work that way.

Not only does a child need both trust and praise, as discussed above, but he also needs limits. A parent is not showing love when he continually supplies the child's desires. In fact, Proverbs says, "Poverty and shame will come to him who neglects discipline" (13:18a).

One way to teach financial discipline is to apply the principle of earned desire. Observe an example.

My oldest son was an avid movie-goer. When he turned 13, he moved from the $1 to the $3.50 admission rate. It was at this point I discussed with him the fact that movies certainly were not a need, and if he wished to continue seeing them, he would have to earn his own way.

After a short period of testing, he decided that I was serious. And if he was going to see a movie, he had better find a way to earn some money. He subsequently found a job mowing our neighbor's lawn. Similar to our home, our neighbor's house is built on a slope so steep that it must be cut while wearing baseball cleats. It took my son nearly three hours to finish the job for which he received the contract price of $3.50.

Later that day, I took him to the movies and picked him up exactly one hour and 30 minutes later. During the ride home, my son shared a profound bit of wisdom when he said, "You know, Dad, I really don't believe movies are a need in my life, either." Since that time, he has become an avid reader and uses his earnings to buy books rather than movies.

Had I commanded my son to stop going to the

movies because they were a waste of money, the result would have been resentment. But he made the decision himself and took an important step in financial responsibility as well.

Mom, Can I Borrow Some Money?

One of the important principles in adolescent financial training is the discipline of repaying. How many times has your son or daughter hit you up for a quick loan when you knew they had neither the means nor inclination to repay?

To give in to them is to teach both deceitfulness and unreliability. You don't think it's that bad? It is. You as a parent set the standards for your children. When you make the rule that your children must earn their money for a particular function, and then neglect to enforce the rule, you are saying to them, "Don't listen to what I say. Make your own plans and I'll do what you want me to when the pressure's on."

Sometimes it may be necessary to advance money. When money is lent, the requirement to repay should be established and enforced. If a written agreement is necessary for "forgetful" offspring, then use one. The discipline you will be imparting to your children will be of lifelong value.

The Adult Child

Stan reflected the lack of early financial training. Though he grew up in affluence, his parents did not lavish toys and other things on him because of the sobering influence of a stern father.

His father suffered a severe heart attack when Stan was about 10, and from that time on, everything changed. Stan was shipped off to a boarding school for a year while his father recovered. Once home, however, he began to pressure his mother for little indulgences to which she acquiesced rather than face an additional crisis.

In high school, Stan continually borrowed money from his mother in direct opposition to his father's wishes. His father, then partially invalided, insisted he pay for some of his own expenses or drop out of school. So under duress Stan took a part-time job. Unfortunately, by this time Stan's routine was established. He would spend his money as he saw fit, then go to his mother under the guise of "borrowing" to meet any other obligations.

In college, Stan began to gamble and had a steady stream of clandestine letters to his mother for "loans" to pay his debts. His dad died before he finished college and from that point on, his mother exercised little or no restraints on his borrowing.

I met Stan when his wife, Peg, dragged him in for help. He not only owed every store and friend in town but also owed several thousand dollars to the local bookies. Several threatening phone calls were all it took to send Peg into panic and push her into a psychiatric clinic.

The breaking point finally came when his mother ran out of money and couldn't bail him out.

One of the things that caught my attention was that Stan could easily trace his decline to his youth and to his mother's indulgence of his irresponsibility. This does not absolve Stan of his own responsibilities, but it does point to the importance of establishing and enforcing financial disciplines for our children.

Rewarding Slothfulness

"In all labor there is profit, but mere talk leads only to poverty" (Prov. 14:23). Take this example:

"Johnny, for the tenth time, you clean your room! This is my last warning! You're not going to the game tonight until you do."

This continues until 7 o'clock that evening when Johnny comes bounding down the stairs as his friends drive up. "Mom, can you let me have some money now? The guys are here." So Mom dips into her purse and rewards Johnny for being such a nice, undisciplined son.

Bribes are a normal part of most American families. The purpose in a bribe is to encourage bothersome kids not to hang around home where parents are constantly reminded that they can't control them.

Very few workers get rewards for sloppy work or jobs left unfinished, and neither should children. Sure, it's tough to tell your child "no" when he's on the way out. Naturally, he won't appreciate it at the time, but the values you establish will remain for a lifetime. "Correct your son, and he will give you comfort; He will also delight your soul" (Prov. 29:17).

But I Want My Kids to Like Me

Many parents try to buy their kids' affection and in so doing abdicate their parental responsibilities. They promise future rewards, allow children adult privileges, or actually allow their children to assume the parents' role in the family. Everything is subordinated to the children's pleasure and approval or disapproval.

There may be several symptoms of this attitude: high school kids in high-powered sportscars; kids with their own charge accounts (paid by the parents); private telephones for the ridiculously long phone calls that Mom can't establish control over.

. . . Do they appreciate this special attention—or lack of it? Hardly. Kids view this for what it usually is: weakness or compromise because of guilt. Then when in real need, they will turn to someone else who has shown both love and discipline.

Guidelines are a necessary part of our lives and our children's lives. Everyone wants to know his boundaries and limitations. Reasonable family rules provide a sense of security.

Observe a young child when he first contacts a new pet such as a puppy. Before play has hardly begun, the child will usually punch, pull, or sit on the puppy. To which the puppy may respond by clamping very sharp teeth around very tender skin. The child cries, the puppy yelps, and the boundaries of the relationship are established. The child will learn to love *and* respect the dog because he knows the dog does not *have* to obey his every wish.

I Can Afford It

The mere presence of enough money to indulge children is not a reason to do so. We as parents have been established as our children's authority, so we are held accountable before the Lord for them.

While particular events in childhood may not be responsible for everything an adult does, it is true that most attitudes and values are the products of parental training.

Establishing Some Reasonable Goals

Is there a scriptural basis for allowances? If there is how should they be managed in the home?

Throughout the Bible, God establishes the parallel between how God deals with us and how we are to deal with our children. "If you then, being evil, know how to give good gifts to your children, how much more shall your Father who is in heaven give what is good to those who ask Him" (Matt. 7:11). Does God give us rewards for being lazy, or sloppy? No, He rewards us for obedience. We should reward our children in the same way.

Establish some minimum standards for your children. If they fail to meet them, there should be a punishment associated. "My son, observe the commandment of your father, and do not forsake the teaching of your mother" (Prov. 6:20). Some of the requirements should be that your children keep their rooms cleaned, their beds made, and their clothes picked off the floor. You also may wish to include such things as getting up on time, brushing their teeth, and dressing themselves. Let your children know that failure to comply with these standards will mean disciplinary action.

One of the most common errors that parents make, however, is to enforce the rules for discipline and punishment but ignore the rewards. Many times parents ask their children to work on a reward basis and then fail to pay them or pay less than agreed upon. To do so only enforces bad habits and attitudes.

Reward your children for extra work around the home. As much as your family budget will allow, your children deserve the equivalent to what you would normally pay an outsider for work done. Some chores you might consider for allowances are cleaning the basement, weeding, house painting, and washing the car. For children who are not particularly strong, you may want to establish other methods for them to earn money. Be careful, however, not to emphasize the differences in ability. Emphasize, rather, that different is not inferior. In these ways, an allowance is not really an allowance, it is pay for tasks performed.

Remember that God has assigned to you as parent the role of teacher, counselor, and benevolent dictator in your home. When your children are undisciplined and untrustworthy with money, God holds *you* responsible. You are *not* responsible for their decisions, but you *are* responsible for their training.

13

A Surplus:

The Great Temptation

Assuming that you have determined to adopt the plans discussed in the previous chapters, you're on your way to peace. For peace doesn't necessarily come when you are out of debt—peace comes when you have made the commitment to get out of debt. For those who are not in debt, it is the commitment to handle money properly.

Both of these commitments require discipline. Discipline on your part means not buying on impulse, particularly with credit cards. Discipline on the part of your children means you need to help them discern between needs, wants, and desires in their own lives. Your responsibility is to meet their needs; their responsibility is to provide for some of their own wants and desires.

Budgeting and planning in your home should not be a chore, but an effort on the part of all members of the family to cooperate in seeking God's best financially.

One of our own early family efforts was to reduce the food expenses in our home. That responsibility did not lie solely with my wife. It also included the rest of us, and it required our cooperation. We approached it as a challenging game with each of us a part of the team.

We exhibited that teamwork one summer when we vacationed in North Carolina. The woman who owned the house next to ours had the largest grape vine I had ever seen. It had grown over the top of a tree and was literally covered with grapes. She was getting ready to return to Florida when my youngest son, Todd (who asks all the questions you always wanted to), asked, "Aren't you going to pick your grapes?"

"No," she said, "I don't have time this year."

So he asked her, "Would you mind if we pick 'em?"

"Not at all," she said. "Help yourselves to all you can get."

At my son's direction we loaded our van full of boxes and loaded the boxes full of grapes.

Once home we converted the grapes into jams, jellies, juices, and purple kids. My kids thought it was great as they squashed grapes, threw grapes, ate grapes, sold grapes, and gave away grapes until we could hardly stand grapes any more. In the process we reduced our overall cost of food very slightly, but at least it was a start.

Use your ingenuity and seek out alternate sources of food that are less expensive. Buy case lots; go to the fields to buy or pick your vegetables if possible. Many times after the professional harvesters have finished a field there will still be food left on the vines. If you are willing to apply your own labor, you can reduce your total budget expense in this area by several hundred dollars a year. I have some of the best bean pickers in Georgia. Given the chance they can strip a field like a swarm of locusts.

When You Almost Have Enough Money For ...

Beware of creeping slothfulness. Watch out for it when you have *almost* enough money for your vacation, your new car, your furniture, or whatever it is that you are saving money for. Stop only when you have enough—not almost enough—money for those things. It is not sufficient to save almost enough money to take a vacation and then use credit cards or borrowed money to make up the difference. It's also not good enough to save almost enough money for new purchases. You must develop the discipline to wait—or risk further financial problems.

One of the characteristics that God is trying to develop in us is patience. "Rest in the Lord and wait patiently for Him" (Ps. 37:7). As discussed earlier, if you will trust God He will provide, whether it's a house, a car, or a vacation.

God used our car to teach my wife and me a lesson of patience and trust. When we left the business world to join the staff of Campus Crusade for Christ, we had a 1969 Lincoln Continental that got three miles to the gallon with the motor off. We began to ask God to supply the car we needed at the price we could afford.

We received $2,500 through a unique set of circumstances in which we sold some stock in a company I had been a part of. We decided that the Lord had supplied us this money specifically to buy the automobile that we needed. We considered big cars and small cars, every kinds of car imaginable until we finally settled on the one we believed would fit all our needs, a Dodge van. We committed to prayer the fact that God would supply us a Dodge van for $2,500.

I don't know how many people have ever looked for a family van less than two years old for $2,500, but such vans are very rare. We looked for nearly seven months during which time we found vans from $3,500 to $7,500, but none even near our requirement.

I had nearly decided that perhaps my leading had been wrong when one day I came out of a meeting with a fellow who got into a Dodge Sportsman Royal Van. I mentioned "I would like to own one like that."

And he replied, "I would really like to sell this one."

So I asked him what he would take for it. To which he replied, "My father bought the van for me two years ago and paid $6,500 for it. I want to get rid of it, and I'll sell it for $4,500."

"I can't go $4,500," I said, "but I do have $2,500." Our conversation ended at that point when I noticed the look of unbelief on his face. I took his card and left.

Two weeks later the Lord put him on my heart, unfortunately, in the middle of the night. I believe when God puts someone on your heart, you should call them. I called and reminded him who I was and asked if he had sold the van.

He said, "You know it's interesting, after I talked to you, my wife and I decided to get serious about selling it. We put it in the newspaper as soon as possible at $3,500. It's a good buy at that price and should have sold quickly. In two weeks we haven't had a single call on the car. Just yesterday my wife and I decided that God had us hold the car for you and we were waiting for you to call us."

"You keep the van, I'll come after it," I replied.

The following Tuesday, we drove over to pick up the vehicle. As I came out of his house, he said, "Do you know what happened? The very next day after I talked to you, I had a dozen calls on that car."

The principle was clear—God was developing an attitude of "trust and obey." When our attitude was aligned to God's, He supplied what we couldn't afford at a price we could. I challenge you to give God an opportunity to supply some of the things you need.

Balance Your Family Life

Giving The first part of your balanced family plan should be to give God the first part of everything that comes into your possession. As God increases your income, increase your giving as well. Do not attempt to bribe God, however, for He cannot be bribed. Paul said, "For who has known the mind of the Lord, or who became His counselor? Or who has first given to Him that it might be paid back to Him again?" (Rom. 11:34-35) It is not our responsibility to tell God, "I need money." God already knows that we need money. We cannot turn on God's plan of giving simply by giving Him some money. God's plan of giving is turned on because He loves us, and because He knows when we can be trusted with an increase. Our giving is the outward reflection of an inner commitment. I challenge you to give God more than you think you can.

Time Balance—God First Bring time into balance in your life. Give God the first part of your life, give your family the second part, and give your work the third part. Your commitment to God entails a minimum discipline in time.

God deserves the best part of your day. Rise early in the morning to read His Word. Pray, for it is through prayer that you can know God. Share, so that you can witness *for* God.

God doesn't need a *quantity* of time. He needs a *quality* of time. I still remember the principle that a pastor shared with me. He said, "Don't try to tell God that you'll give him two hours a day, because you can't do that. Don't tell God you'll give Him an hour a day, because you won't do that either." The plan he started me on was called the 9-59 plan. Nine minutes and 59 seconds a day alone with God. He said, "If you stick to this plan it will revolutionize your life."

It will. You'll quickly find that you can't spend just nine minutes and 59 seconds a day alone with God.

Time Balance—Family Second Give your family the next part of your day. Husband and wife need to spend time together. The commitment a husband has, next to God, is to his wife. The two of you must set aside some time on a regular basis in order to communicate and get to know each other.

The next portion of your lives belongs to your children. Parents need time to train children and teach them God's Word. Set aside time on a regular basis to read the Bible with your family. Ask them questions and allow them a chance to ask questions.

You will get to know more about your children in a 30-minute Bible study and sharing time than you will in 15 hours watching television together.

Time Balance—Work Third Your third commitment is to your work. You should give yourself wholeheartedly to your work. God established the principle that Christians are to excel at what they do. "Whatever you do, do your work heartily, as for the Lord rather than for men" (Col. 3:23).

Christians are also admonished by God to give honor to the authority above us. "Therefore he who resists authority has opposed the ordinance of God; and they who have opposed will receive condemnation upon themselves" (Romans 13:2).

Women in the home need to establish the same principles. Your home should be so clean, well-organized, and disciplined that when a neighbor comes over to visit, it will be a visible witness for the Lord Jesus Christ. Never give into the "Oh-I'm-just-a-housewife" attitude. Homemaking happens to be one of the most important jobs that God ever assigned to anyone.

Levels of Growth

There are several levels of growth for anything that you can attempt. Many families are operating financially at the bottom level, borrowing money for virtually everything. God wants us to operate at the uppermost level, totally depending on Him for everything we need. We cannot move from the bottom to the top levels in one step. Instead, move from level one to level two, which might mean that you stop borrowing for small purchases, particularly consumables. Once you have that under control, move to the next level, not borrowing for larger purchases such as major appliances. And so on.

Many families don't know, for instance, that they can own their home sooner than they thought possible. If the average family could apply $100 a month extra to their mortgage payment, in about 12 years they would own their home debt-free. The first payment made each month goes monthly to interest with only a small portion going to principle.

The second payment of $100 would go entirely to principle. So in approximately 12 years, a $35,000 mortgage would be paid in full.

Avoid Complacency

One of the inherent dangers in any budget is complacency. One of the indications that complacency has set in is when your bankbook doesn't quite balance anymore. Nip it in the bud. Never leave your balance in error, not even a single cent.

Another sign of complacency is when you abandon your budget, and forget the details about how much is spent and why! You must be aware of how much you are spending on your home, groceries, car, insurance, clothes, everything. Otherwise you'll end up right back where you started, saying, "Where did all the money go again?"

Ignorance is not bliss. It is a headache. If you find that your old habits have returned, stop right where you are! Reinstate your budget and discipline yourself to sticking to it.

Keep Your Finances Current

Beware of the temptation to follow others, even your closest friends. In some circles we have observed that private schools are one source of overspending almost unique to Christians. Don't be swayed by social pressures that demand Christian parents to send their children to Christian schools. If God has provided the money within your budget, consider it a blessing from Him. If, however, God has not done so, believe that He has other priorities.

College bills are another factor that can wreck your budget regardless of the debt situation. You should encourage your children to live within your budget. If you can only provide half of their college expenses, then you should trust that God has another plan for the other half. Perhaps He wants them to work for a portion of their education.

Perhaps the most common budget-breaker is an extra automobile. It may be the second car for the wife or the third car for the children. Either way, an additional car represents an additional expense. If your children need a car, allow them to earn it. But better than that, pray earnestly about whether they should even have a car. Not only does it generate additional expenses to maintain the car, they are no longer as free as before. At best a car will always be an interference in their lives. It is you who is responsible before the Lord. Accept that responsibility.

Another temptation you must avoid is the new house syndrome. Once you're out of debt and have a surplus of money it is easy to become overconfident. Stick with your plans to fix your spending level and allow God to adjust your standard of living.

Avoid the Hoarding Trap

One of the indications that you've fallen into the hoarding trap is if your giving begins to slack off. If you find that you're no longer as eager to give to others as you were before, you are developing into a hoarder.

Another indication is saving without purpose. Remember the difference between hoarding and saving? Savings must have a purpose. But if you begin saving for some elusive rainy day, it no longer has a purpose and thus qualifies as hoarding.

Another indication of hoarding is when family needs are sacrificed just to save money. Many men get so carried away by their zeal to save that family needs go wanting. Remember the principle: "So is the man who lays up treasure for himself, and is not rich toward God" (Luke 12:21).

Family Goals—Conclusion

Continue your life notebook. Use it to record your financial successes. This will be one of your greatest sources of spiritual encouragement when problems arise, and arise they will. Satan does not give up easily. You can expect some testing of your commitment to operate totally under God's authority. Stay with your spiritual goals regardless of the periodic difficulties.